Dorothy B. Porter

North American Negro Poets

North American Negro Poets

Poets

A Bibliographical Checklist
of Their Writings
1760-1944

BY
DOROTHY B. PORTER

THE BOOK FARM
HATTIESBURG, MISSISSIPPI
1945

HEARTMAN'S HISTORICAL SERIES No. 70

Copyright
THE BOOK FARM
Hattiesburg, Mississippi
1945

PREFACE

In 1916, Arthur Alfonso Schomburg, well-known collector and curator, published the first considerable bibliography of American Negro poetry*. In this compilation were listed 236 titles with a bibliography of some 38 editions of the poetry of Phillis Wheatley compiled earlier by Charles F. Heartman. In addition to the writings of Negro poets of the United States, there was a small group of titles from persons of Negro ancestry of Cuba, Haiti, Puerto Rico and Jamaica.

The present bibliography is an expansion of the Schomburg checklist. While it does not include the foreign titles of the earlier list it more than doubles the number of domestic titles alone which were listed in the Schomburg list. This list includes, specifically, books and pamphlets by individual poets: anthologies edited by Negro authors and a few printed broadsides. It also presents some occasional poems which were originally appended to or included in prose writings prior to 1835. If I reiterate that this bibliography primarily contains works by Negro authors born in the United States it is only to disclose that the exception thereto is a number of works by West Indian writers who have lived an appreciable time in the United States or who have had their works published here in the English Language.

It must be mentioned that one of the principal objectives of this bibliography is to afford an index to the relative distribution of books and other published materials of Negro poetry among our libraries and thus indirectly to reflect the richness of American holdings in this sphere. It was not the compiler's aim, however, to make this an exhaustive bibliography; some titles have escaped the attention of the compiler; others known to have been printed could not be located. It is hoped that omissions or corrections when determined by the reader will be forwarded to the compiler. The exclusion of editions of Negro poetry translated into foreign languages and of new editions or translations of classics or other works

---

*Arthur A. Schomburg. A Bibliographical Checklist of American Negro Poetry. New York, Charles F. Heartman, 1916. 57 pages.

previously published was decided upon for reasons of economy and brevity and directness. It was also recognized that a checklist of titles culled from periodical literature of both this and an earlier day would have been very desirable, although at the present time too involved a task to be merely inserted as filling for the present work.

As to the usefulness of a bibliography of Negro poetry, the very fact that the need for revision and expansion of the earlier compilation by Schomburg has been recognized is sufficient testimony. Certainly there is no reason to regard the olden question, "Is poetry racial?" a valid objection to this enterprise, since it has been shown that a poem can be racial in content while remaining poetic in form. And it is for those who may wish to study the facets of race consciousness in Negro expression as well as the aesthetic factors that this bibliography is intended.

The compiler wishes to acknowledge indebtedness to the Librarians of the Schomburg Collection, 135th Street Public Library, New York City, and to Miss Gertrude Franklin, cataloger at Lincoln University Library, Lincoln, Mo. Miss Franklin was kind enough to verify certain volumes in the library of Atlanta University which were not found elsewhere. To Mr. Henry P. Slaughter of Washington, D. C.; Mr. Arthur B. Spingarn of New York City, and Mr. Charles F. Heartman of Hattiesburg, Miss., well-known collectors of Negroana, special acknowledgements are due for their willingness to open the resources of their collections to the compiler. The entries of the Writings of Phillis Wheatley have been reprinted from Mr. C. F. Heartman's Bibliography of Phillis Wheatley with his permission.

Howard University   DOROTHY B. PORTER
Washington, D. C.
December 30, 1944.

NOTE

Key to symbols indicating the location of the volumes of poetry included.

ABSpl   Arthur B. Spingarn private library, New York City

AAS   American Antiquarian Society, Worcester, Mass.

AU   Atlanta University Library, Atlanta, Ga.

BA   Boston Athenaeum, Boston, Mass.

BPL   Boston Public Library, Boston, Mass.

BU   Boston University, Boston, Mass.

CFH   C. Fiske Harris Collection, Providence, R. I.

CHS   Connecticut Historical Society, Hartford, Conn.

DHU   Howard University Library, Washington, D. C.

DLC   The Library of Congress, Washington, D. C.

EMCpl   Edward M. Coleman private library, Washington, D. C.

HCL   Harvard College Library, Cambridge, Mass.

HE   Charles F. Heartman Collection, Hattiesburg, Miss.

HPBpl   Hilda P. Brawley private library, Washington, D. C.

HPSpl   Henry P. Slaughter private library, Washington, D. C.

JCB   John Carter Brown Library, Providence, R. I.

LCP   Library Company, Philadelphia, Pa.

LCRB   Library Company, Ridgway Branch, Philadelphia, Pa.

MHS   Massachusetts Historical Society, Boston, Mass.

NYHS   New York Historical Society, New York City.

NYPL   New York Public Library, New York City.

NYPLS   New York Public Library, Schomburg Collection, New York City.

PHS   Pennsylvania Historical Society, Philadelphia, Pa.

SABpl   Sterling A. Brown private library, Washington, D. C.

YU   Yale University Library, New Haven, Conn.

ADAMS, WELLINGTON ALEXANDER.
    Lyrics of an Humble Birth, by Wellington Adams. Wash-
    ington, D. C., Murray Brothers Printing Co., 1914.
    48 pages. Portrait.
    DHU DLC HPSpl

ALDEBARAN, Pseud. See Byer, A. P.

ALLEN, JUNIUS MORECAI.
    Rhymes, Tales and Rhymed Tales, by J. Mord. Allen.
    Topeka, Kansas: Monotyped by Crane and Co., 1906.
    153 pages.
    ABSpl DHU NYPLS

ANDERSON, ANITA TURPEAU.
    Penpoints Group of Poems and Prose Writings. Fairmont
    Heights, Md., Published by Campbell Press, 1943.
    20 pages.
    DHU

ANDREWS, HENRY H.
    Idle Moments. New York, Poets Press, 1941.
    50 pages.
    ABSpl

ANDREWS, HENRY H.
    Vicious Youth. A Poem by Henry Andrews. Boston Popu-
    lar Poetry Publishers. (1940).
    34 pages.
    ABSpl DHU

ANDUZE, AUBREY.
    Reminiscence, by Aubrey Anduze. St. Thomas, Virgin Is-
    land, The Art Shop, 1940.
    89 pages.
    ABSpl

ATKINS, THOMAS.
    The Eagle by Thomas Atkins_____St. Louis, Published by
    the St. Louis Argus, 1936.
    87 pages. Portrait.
    ABSpl

BANKS, WILLIAM AUGUSTUS.
    "Gathering Dusk," by William Augustus Banks. Chatta-
    nooga, Tenn., The Wilson Printing Company (c1935).
    8 pages.
    ABSpl

9

BANKS, WILLIAM AUGUSTUS.
"Lest We Forget." By William Augustus Banks. Chatta-
nooga, Tenn., Central High Press (1930).
11 pages.
ABSpl

BATIPPS, PERCY OLIVER.
Lines of Life, by Percy Oliver Batipps. Media, Penn.,
American Publishing Co., 1924.
118 pages.
DLC HPSpl

(BATSON, FLORA).
Life, Travels and Works of Miss Flora Batson, Deceased
Queen of Song, by Gerard Millar the Basso, for ten years
her manager and professional associate, interspersed with
comments from the leading characters of the world, and
original poems heretofore unpublished. Published by
T.M.R.M. Company, Gerard Millar, Manager. N.d.
92 pages.
HPSpl NYPLS

BATTLE, EFFIE T.
Gleanings from Dixie Land. (Typesetting and Presswork
done by Students of the Tuskegee Normal and Industrial
Institute, Alabama.) (N.d.)
24 pages.
ABSpl NYPLS

BATTLE, EFFIE T.
Gleanings from Dixie-land in Ten Poems. Okolona, Miss.,
The Author (189-?).
17 pages. Portrait.
NYPLS

BAXTER, JOSEPH HARVEY LOWELL.
Sonnets for the Ethiopians and Other Poems, by Joseph
Harvey L. Baxter. Roanoke, Va., The Magic City Press,
1936.
DHU DLC HPSpl ABSpl

BAXTER, JOSEPH HARVEY LOWELL.
That Which Concerneth Me. Sonnets and Other Poems,
by Joseph Harvey L. Baxter. Roanoke, Va., Published by
the Magic City Press, 1934.
87 pages.
ABSpl DHU DLC HE HPSpl

BEADLE, SAMUEL ALFRED.
Lyrics of the Under World, by S. A. Beadle. Jackson, Miss.,
W. A. Scott, publisher. 1912. Portrait.
148 pages.
ABSpl DLC HPSpl NYPLS

BELL, JAMES MADISON.
An Anniversary Poem Entitled The Progress of Liberty. Delivered January 1st, 1866, at Zion Church at the Celebration of the Third Anniversary of President Lincoln's Proclamation. San Francisco, Agnew & Deffeback, Printers, 511 Street cor. Merchant, 1866.
28 pages.
NYPLS

BELL, JAMES MADISON.
A Poem Entitled The Day and the War, Delivered January 1, 1864, at Platt's Hall by J. Madison Bell at the Celebration of the First Anniversary of President Lincoln's Emancipation Proclamation. San Francisco, Agnew and Deffebach, Printers, 1864.
27 pages.
ABSpl DLC

BELL, JAMES MADISON.
A Poem, Entitled the Triumph of Liberty, Delivered April 7, 1870, at Detroit Opera House, by J. Madison Bell, on the Occasion of the Fifteenth Amendment to the Constitution of the United States. Detroit, Printed by the Tunis Steam Printing Co., 1870.
32 pages. Portrait.
ABSpl NYPLS

BELL, JAMES MADISON.
The Poetical Works of James Madison Bell. Lansing, Michigan, Press of Wynkoop, Hallenbeck, Crawford Co., (c1901).
208 pages. Portrait.
DHU DLC HPDpl

BELL, JAMES MADISON.
The Poetical Works of James Madison Bell, 2d ed. Lansing, Michigan, Press of Wynkoop, Hallenbeck, Crawford Co., (c1901).
221(1) pages. Portrait.
APSpl

BENJAMIN, ROBERT C. O.
Poetic Gems, by Robert C. O. Benjamin. Charlottesville, Va., Peck and Allan, 1883.
14 pages.
DLC HE NYPLS

BERRY, LLOYD ANDREW.
Heart Songs and Bygones, by Lloyd Andrew Berry. Dayton, Ohio, Lloyd Andrew Berry, 1926.
40 pages. Portrait.
ABSpl

11

BIBB, ELOISE.
Poems, by Eloise Bibb. Boston, Mass., The Monthly Review Press., (c1895).
107 pages.
ABSpl DLC HE NYPLS

BIDDLE, WILLIAM T.
The Carol of Zion, Original and Selected by Wm. T. Biddle. For Use in All Religious Services. (No Imprint).
32(2) pages.
HPSpl

BIRD, BESSIE CALHOUN.
Airs from the Wood-Winds, by Bessie Calhoun Bird, with an Introduction by Arthur Huff Fauset. Philadelphia, Pa., Alpress (c1935).
23 pages.
Edition of 300 copies on Covenant Book Paper.
ABSpl

BLADES, WILLIAM C.
Negro Poems, Melodies, Plantation Negro Pieces, Camp Meeting Songs, by William C. Blades. Boston, Richard J. Badger, The Gorman Press (c1921).
ABSpl DLC HPSpl

BLAKELEY, AL ETHELRED.
Poetic Facts and Philosophy, by Al Ethelred Blakeley. New York, Al Ethelred Blakeley and Co., publishers, 1963 Seventh Ave., c1936.
23 pages..   Pages 21-23 are prose.
ABSpl HE

BONTEMPS, ARNA, COMP.
Golden Slippers. An Anthology of Negro Poetry for Young Readers, compiled by Arna Bontemps, with Drawings by Henrietta Bruce Sharon. New York and London, Harper and Brothers, 1941.
220 pages.
ABSpl DHU DLC HPSpl NYPLS

BORDERS, WILLIAM HOLMES.
Thunderbolts. (Atlanta, Ga., Morris Brown College Press, 1942.)
50 pages.
ABSpl HPSpl

(BOWLES, LILLIAN MAE).
Bowles Book of Poems for All Occasions with Welcome Addresses and responses, ed. by Charles R. Saulter, q Chicago, Ill., Bowles Music House, n.d.
34(1) pages. Portrait.
HPSpl

BOYD, R. F.
   Holiday Stanzas. New York, Fortuny's (c1940).
   93 pages. Portrait.
   ABSpl

BRAITHWAITE, WILLIAM STANLEY BAUMONT.
   Anthology of Magazine Verse for 1913, including the Maga-
   zines and the Poets; a Review by William Stanley Braithwaite. Cambridge, Mass., issued by W.S.B. (c1913). XIII.
   87 pages.
   ABSpl DHU DLC HE HPSpl NYPLS

BRAITHWAITE, WILLIAM STANLEY BAUMONT, ED.
   Anthology of Magazine verse for 1914 and Yearbook of
   American Poetry, edited by William Stanley Braithwaite.
   Cambridge, Massachusetts, issued by W.S.B., (c1914.) XXIV.
   205 pages.
   ABSpl DHU   HE HPSpl NYPLS

BRAITHWAITE, WILLIAM STANLEY BAUMONT, ED.
   Anthology of Magazine Verse for 1914 and Yearbook of
   American Poetry, edited by William Stanley Braithwaite.
   New York, Laurence J. Gomme, 1914.
   205 pages.
   ABSpl DHU HPSpl NYPLS

BRAITHWAITE, WILLIAM STANLEY BAUMONT, ED.
   Anthology of Magazine Verse for 1915 and Yearbook of
   American Poetry, edited by William Stanley Braithwaite.
   New York, Laurence J. Gomme, 1915.
   28, 296 pages.
   DHU HE HPSpl NYPLS ABSpl

BRAITHWAITE, WILLIAM STANLEY BAUMONT, ED.
   Anthology of Magazine Verse for 1915 and Yearbook of
   American Poetry, edited by William Stanley Braithwaite.
   New York, Gomme and Marshall, 1915.
   28, 296 pages.
   DHU HE HPSpl NYPLS

BRAITHWAITE, WILLIAM STANLEY BAUMONT, ED.
   Anthology of Magazine Verse for 1916 and Yearbook of
   American Poetry, edited by William Stanley Braithwaite.
   New York, Laurence J. Gomme, 1916.
   XX, 266 pages.
   DHU HE HPSpl NYPLS

BRAITHWAITE, WILLIAM STANLEY BAUMONT, ED.
   Anthology of Magazine Verse for 1917 and Yearbook of
   American Poetry, edited by William Stanley Braithwaite.
   Boston, Small, Maynard and Company, Publishers, 1917.
   XXVII, 412 pages.
   ABSpl DHU HE HPDpl NYPLS

13

BRAITHWAITE, WILLIAM STANLEY BAUMONT, ED.
Anthology of Magazine Verse for 1918 and Yearbook of
American Poetry, edited by William Stanley Braithwaite.
Boston, Small, Maynard and Company, Publishers, 1918.
23, 285 pages.
ABSpl DHU HE HPDpl NYPLS

BRAITHWAITE, WILLIAM STANLEY BAUMONT, ED.
Anthology of Magazine Verse for 1919 and Yearbook of
American Poetry, edited by William Stanley Braithwaite.
Boston, Small, Maynard and Company Publishers, 1919.
77, 320 pages.
ABSpl DHU HE HPSpl NYPLS

BRAITHWAITE, WILLIAM STANLEY BAUMONT, ED.
Anthology of Magazine Verse for 1920 and Yearbook of
American Poetry, edited by William Stanley Baumont
Braithwaite. Boston, Small, Maynard and Company Pub-
lishers, 1920.
XII, 182 pages.
ABSpl DHU HE HPSpl NYPLS

BRAITHWAITE, WILLIAM STANLEY BAUMONT, ED.
Anthology of Magazine Verse for 1921 and Year Book of
American Poetry, edited by William Stanley Braithwaite.
Boston, Small, Maynard and Company Publishers, 1921.
13, 294 pages.
ABSpl DHU HE HPSpl NYPLS

BRAITHWAITE, WILLIAM STANLEY BAUMONT, ED.
Anthology of Magazine Verse for 1922 and Yearbook of
American Poetry, edited by William Stanley Braithwaite.
Boston, Small, Maynard and Company, Publishers (c1923).
XXVI, 387 pages.
ABSpl DHU HE HPSpl NYPLS

BRAITHWAITE, WILLIAM STANLEY BAUMONT, ED.
Annthology of Magazine Verse for 1923 and Yearbook of
American Poetry, edited by William Stanley Braithwaite.
Boston, B. J. Brimmer Company, 1923.
XIX, 376, 188 pages.
ABSpl HE HPSpl NYPLS

BRAITHWAITE, WILLIAM STANLEY BAUMONT, ED.
Anthology of Magazine Verse for 1925 and Yearbook of
American Poetry, edited by William Stanley Braithwaite.
Boston, B. J. Brimmer Company, 1925.
XXXIV, 383, 208 pages.
ABSpl HE HPSpl NYPLS

BRAITHWAITE, WILLIAM STANLEY BANMONT, ED.
Anthology of Magazine Verse for 1926 and Yearbook of
American Poetry. (Sesqui-Centennial Edition), edited by
William Stanley Braithwaite. Boston, B. J. Brimmer Com-
pany, 1926.
XXXI, 496, 171, 43 pages.
ABSpl   HE   HPSpl   NYPLS   DHU

BRAITHWAITE, WILLIAM STANLEY BAUMONT, ED.
Anthology of Magazine Verse for 1927 and Yearbook of
American Poetry, edited by William Stanley Braithwaite.
Boston, B. J. Brimmer, 1927.
XXIV, 405, 146 pages.
ABSpl   DHU   HE   HPSpl   NYPLS

BRAITHWAITE, WILLIAM STANLEY BAUMONT, ED.
Anthology of Magazine Verse for 1928 and Yearbook of
American Poetry, Edited by William Stanley Braithwaite.
New York, Harold Vinal, 1928.
XXIV, 697 pages.
ABSpl   HE   HPSpl   NYPLS

BRAITHWAITE, WILLIAM STANLEY BAUMONT, ED.
Anthology of Magazine Verse for 1929 and Yearbook of
American Poetry, Edited by William Stanley Braithwaite.
New York, George Sully and Company, Inc., 1929.
XXXIX, 677 pages.
ABSpl   HE   HPSpl   NYPLS

BRAITHWAITE, WILLIAM STANLEY BAUMONT, ED.
Anthology of Massachusetts Poets by William Stanley
Braithwaite. Boston, Small, Maynard and Company, Pub-
lishers, 1922.
145 pages.
ABSpl   DHU   HPSpl

BRAITHWAITE, WILLIAM STANLEY BAUMONT, ED.
The Book of Elizabethan Verse, Chosen and Edited with
notes, by William Stanley Braithwaite, with an introduction by Thomas Wentworth Higginson. Boston, H. B. Turner
and Company, 1906.
787 pages.
ABSpl   DLC   HPSpl

BRAITHWAITE, WILLIAM STANLEY BAUMONT, ED.
The Book of Elizabethan Verse, Chosen and Edited with
notes, by William Stanley Braithwaite; with an introduction by Thomas Wenthorth Higginson. 2nd ed. Boston, H.
B. Turner and Co., 1907.
823 pages.
ABSpl   DLC   NYPLS

BRAITHWAITE, WILLIAM STANLEY BAUMONT, ED.

The Book of Elizabethan Verse, Chosen and Editen with notes by William Stanley Braithwaite. London, Chatto and Winders, 1908.
823 pages.
ABSpl DLC

BRAITHWAITE, WILLIAM STANLEY BAUMONT, ED.

The Book of Georgian Verse, chosen and edited with notes by William Stanley Braithwaite. New York, Brentano's, 1909.
1313 pages.
ABSpl DLC DPSpl NYPLS

BRAITHWAITE, WILLIAM STANLEY BAUMONT, ED.

The Book of Georgian Verse, chosen and edited, with notes, by William Stanley Braithwaite. London, Duckworth and Co. (c1914).
1313 pages.
DLC ABSpl

BRAITHWAITE, WILLIAM STANLEY BAUMONT, ED.

The Book of Modern British Verse, edited by William Stanley Braithwaite. Boston, Small, Maynard and Co., (c1919).
270 pages.
ABSpl DLC

BRAITHWAITE, WILLIAM STANLEY BAUMONT, ED.

The Book of Restoration Verse, chosen and edited with notes, by William Stanley Braithwaite. New York, Brentano's, 1910.
864 pages.
ABSpl DLC HPSpl NYPLS

BRAITHWAITE, WILLIAM STANLEY BAUMONT, ED.

The Book of Restoration Verse, chosen and edited with notes by William Stanley Braithwaite. London, Duckworth and Co., n.d.
864 pages.
ABSpl

BRAITHWAITE, WILLIAM STANLEY BAUMONT, ED.

The Golden Treasury of Magazine Verse, edited by William Stanley Braithwaite. Boston, Small, Maynard and Company (c1918).
XX, 324 pages.
ABSpl DHU DLC HE HPSpl NYPLS

BRAITHWAITE, WILLIAM STANLEY BAUMONT, ED.
    The House of Falling Leaves, With Other Poems by Wil-
    liam Stanley Braithwaite. Boston, John W. Luce and Com-
    pany, 1908.
    112 pages.
    ABSpl   DHU   HPSpl   NYPLS

BRAITHWAITE, WILLIAM STANLEY BAUMONT.
    Lyrics of Life and Love, by William Stanley Braithwaite.
    Boston, Herbert B. Turner and Company, 1904.
    80 pages. Portrait.
    ABSpl   DHU   HPSpl   NYPLS

BRAITHWAITE, WILLIAM STANLEY BAUMONT, ED.
    Our Lady's Choir; A Contemporary Anthology of Verse
    by Catholic Sisters, edited by William Stanley Braithwaite,
    with a foreword by the Rev. Hugh Francis Blunt and an
    introduction by Ralph Adams Cram. Boston, Bruce Hum-
    phries, Inc., 1931.
    213 pages.
    Limited edition of which there were:
    25 copies on sheepskin (1-25)
    50 copies on Kelmscott hand-made paper (26-75)
    500 copies on Worthy Hand and Arrows paper (76-755)
    2000 copies on Hamilton's Mellow Book (not numbered)
    ABSpl (132)   DHU   DLC   HPSpl   NYPLS

BRAITHWAITE, WILLIAM STANLEY BAUMONT, ED.
    Our Lady's Choir, A Contemporary Anthology of Verse by
    Catholic Sisters Edited by William Stanley Braithwaite
    with a Foreword by The Rev. Hugh Francis Blunt and an
    introduction by Ralph Adams Cram, Litt.D. Boston, Bruce
    Humphries, Inc. 1938.
    XXX, 210 pages.
    HE

BRAITHWAITE, WILLIAM STANLEY BAUMONT, ED.
    The Poetic Year of 1916; A Critical Anthology by William
    Stanley Braithwaite. Boston, Small, Maynard and Com-
    pany (c1917).
    191, 403 pages.
    ABSpl   DLC   DHU   HE   HPSpl   NYPLS

BRAITHWAITE, WILLIAM STANLEY BAUMONT, ED.
    Representative American Poetry, edited by William Stan-
    ley Braithwaite and Henry Thomas Scknittkind. Boston, R.
    G. Badger (c1916).
    30 pages.
    ABSpl   DLC   HPSpl

BRAITHWAITE, WILLIAM STANLEY BAUMONT, ED.
A Tale of a Walled Town and other Verses by B. 8266
_____Penitentiary. With An Introduction by William Stanley Braithwaite. Philadelphia and London. J. B. Lippincott Company, 1921.
121 pages.
HE

BRAITHWAITE, WILLIAM STANLEY BAUMONT, ED.
Victory! Celebrated by Thirty-Eight American Poets, brought together by William Stanley Braithwaite, with an introduction by Theodore Roosevelt. Boston, Small, Maynard and Company Publishers, (1919).
VIII, 84 pages.
ABSpl   DHU   HE   HPDpl   NYPLS

BRAWLEY, BENJAMIN GRIFFITH.
The Dawn and Other Poems. (No imprint, 1912). 6 unnumbered leaves.
HPB   pl

BRAWLEY, BENJAMIN GRIFFITH.
The Desire of the Moth for the Star. Atlanta, Ga., Privately Printed, 1906.
10 pages.
ABSpl   NYPLS

BRAWLEY, BENJAMIN GRIFFITH, COMP.
Howard University Songs, compiled by Benjamin Griffith Brawley. (No imprint.) 1912.
10 pages.
DHU

BRAWLEY, BENJAMIN GRIFFITH.
Poems. (No imprint). (10) leaves.
AU

BRAWLEY, BENJAMIN GRIFFITH.
A Prayer, Words by B. G. Brawley _____ (Atlanta, Ga.) Atlanta Baptist College (1899).
6 pages.
The poem has been set to music by A. H. Ryder.
ABSpl

BRAWLEY, BENJAMIN GRIFFITH.
The Problem and Other Poems, by Benjamin Griffith Brawley (four lines of verse). Atlanta, Ga., Atlanta Baptist College Print (1905).
18 pages.
DLC   HPSpl   NYPLS

BRAWLEY, BENJAMIN GRIFFITH.
  The Seven Sleepers of Ephesus. A lyrical legend by Benjamin Brawley. (Atlanta, Ga., Foote and Davies. c1917).
  8 pages.
  NYPLS

BRAWLEY, BENJAMIN GRIFFITH.
  A Toast to Love and Death, Atlanta, Ga., Privately Printed, 1902.
  29 pages.
  ABSpl   NYPLS

BREWER, JOHN MASON.
  Echoes of Thought, by John Mason Brewer. (Fort Worth, Texas. Progressive Printing Company, c1922).
  54 pages. Portrait.
  DLC

BREWER, JOHN MASON.
  Heralding Dawn, an Anthology of Verse, by (1) Selected, with a Historical Summary on the Texas Negroes, versemaking by John Mason Brewer and with a preface by Henry Smith.   Dallas, Texas, June Thomason, Printing, 1936.
  45 pages.
  DLC   HE

BREWER, JOHN MASON.
  The Life of John Wesley Anderson _____ in verse, by John Mason Brewer. (Dallas, Tex., Printed by C. C. Cockrell & Son, c1938).
  108, 23 pages. Portrait.
  DHU   DLC

BREWER, JOHN MASON.
  Negrito, Negro Dialect Poems of the Southwest, by J. Mason Brewer with illustrations by Tom Smith.   San Antonio, Texas, Naylor Printing Company, 1933.
  97, (1) pages.
  ABSpl   DHU   DLC   HE

BREWER, JOHN MASON, ED.
  Patriotic Moments. A Second Book of Verse by the Bellerophon Quill Club of The Booker T. Washington High School, Dallas, Texas, ed. by J. Mason Brewer.   1936. (n.p.n.d.)
  24 pages.
  ABSpl

BREWER, JOHN MASON, ED.
Senior Sentiments and Junior Jottings. A First Book of Verse by The Bellerophon Quill Club of the Booker T. Washington High School. Dallas, Texas, ed. by J. Mason Brewer, 1934.
24 pages.
ABSpl

BROOKS, WALTER HENDERSON.
A Black Man's Soliloquy—Right Wins the Day. (No imprint).
Broadside, 13x21½cm.
DHU

BROOKS, WALTER HENDERSON.
Original Poems, by Rev. Walter H. Brooks. Published by the Sunday School of the Church in Connection with the Fiftieth Anniversary of his Service as Pastor. Washington, D. C., 1932.
40 pages. Portrait.
ABSpl DHU HPSpl NYPLS

BROOKS, W. H.
The Schomburg edition has: Ode of Welcome to Frederick Douglass which could not be located.

BROWN, HATTIE.
Catoninetas. A Domestic Epic by Hattie Brown, a young lady of Color. Lately deceased at the age of 14. London, 1891. This title was reported to C. F. Heartman.

BROWN, SAMUEL E.
Love Letters in Rhyme, by Samuel E. Brown. New York, Published by Samuel E. Brown (c1930).
29 pages.
ABSpl

BROWN, SOLOMON G.
Congratulations to Solomon G. Brown. A Verse—Fifty Years To-Day. This Verse Written at Request of Several Friends Commemorative of An Official Visit made to Solomon G. Brown, on the Morning of February 15th, 1902, by the Secretary of Smithsonian Institution, Washinigton, D. C., Smithsonian Institute, 1902.
(3)pp.
DHU

BROWN, SOLOMON G.
"He is a Negro Still." The Uncompromising Prejudice Towards the Negro American. A Reply. (No imprint).
(4)pp.
DHU

BROWN, SOLOMON G.
Our Church Entertainments. Verse Prepared and Read at
the Prize Literary Meeting at Hillsdale Station C. M. E.
Church by Special Invitation, January 16th, 1893. Hillsdale, D. C., February 10th, 1893.
(3)pp.
DHU

BROWN, SOLOMON G.
"My Husband Sells Whisky, But What Can I Do?" (But
Few Know the Sorrows of the Saloon-Keeper's Wife.) Dedi-
cated to the Junior Grand Lodge of Independent Order of
Good Templars for the District of Columbia. (No imprint).
November, 1890.
(2)pp.
DHU

BROWN, SOLOMON G.
"What Brings Me to This Lonely Place, Nowhere a Home."
After an Absence of One Million Years, One Returns and
is Greatly Surprised at the Wonderful Changes that have
taken place in Such Time. Washington, D. C., 1896.
8pp.
DHU

BROWN, STERLING ALLEN.
Southern Road, by Sterling A. Brown. New York, Harcourt,
Brace and Company, 1932.
142 pages.
ABSpl   DHU   DLC   HPSpl   NYPLS

BROWN THRUSH, THE.
The Brown Thrush, Anthology of Verse by Negro Students,
edited by Lillian W. Voorhees and Robert W. O'Brien.
Bryn Athyn, Pa., Claremont, California, Lauson-Roberts
Publishing Company, 1932.   Volume I.
ABSpl   DHU   DLC   NYPLS

BROWN THRUSH, THE.
The Brown Thrush, Anthology of Verse by Negro Students.
Edited by Helen O'Brien, Lillian W. Voorhees and Hugh M.
Gloster. Memphis, Tenn., The Malcom-Roberts Publishing
Company, 1935.   Volume II.
ABSpl   DLC   NYPLS

BROWN, WILLIAM WELLS, COMP.
Anti-Slavery Harp; a Collection of Songs for Anti-Slavery
Meetings, compiled by William W. Brown. Boston, Pub-
lished by Bela Marsh, 1848.
47(1) pages.
ABSpl   DHU

21

BROWN, WILLIAM WELLS, COMP.
    Anti-Slavery Harp; a Collection of Songs for Anti-Slavery
    Meetings, compiled by William W. Brown, 2d ed. Boston,
    Published by Bela Marsh, 1849.
    48 pages.
    DLC   HPSpl   NYPLS

BROWNLEE, JULIUS PINKNEY.
    Ripples, by J. P. Brownlee. Anderson, S. C., Cox Stationery
    Co., 1914.
    48 pages. Portrait.
    DLC   NYPLS

BRYANT, FRANKLIN HENRY.
    Black Smiles; or, The Sunny Side of Sable Life, by Frank-
    lin Henry Bryant. Nashville, Tenn., Blackport Studio (1903).
    56 pages. Portrait.
    DLC   HE

BRYANT, FRANKLIN HENRY.
    Black Smiles; or, the Sunny Side of Sable Life, by Franklin
    Henry Bryant. Nashville, Tenn., Southern Missionary So-
    ciety (1909).
    57 pages. Portrait.
    NYPLS

BRYSON, CLARENCE F. AND ROBINSON, J. H.
    Dundo; Anthology of Cleveland Negro Youth, edited by
    Clarence F. Bryson and James H. Robinson. Cleveland,
    Ohio, The January Club, 1931.
    76 pages.
    DHU   DLC   NYPLS

BURRELL, LOUIS V.
    The Petals of the Rose; Poems and Epigrams, by Louis V.
    Burrell. Morton, (Del. Co.) Pa., V. Burrell (1917).
    55 pages. Portrait.
    DLC   NYPLS

BUSH, OLIVIA WARD.
    Driftwood, by Olivia Ward Bush. (Providence, R. I., Atlan-
    tic Printing Co. c1914.
    86(1) pages.
    ABSpl

BUTLER, ALPHEUS.
    Make Way for Happiness, by Alpheus Butler. Boston, The
    Christopher Publishing House, (c1932).
    133 pages.
    ABSpl   DHU   DLC   HPSpl   NYPLS

BUTLER, ALPHEUS.
Sepia Vistas, by Alpheus Butler. New York. The Exposition Press, 1941.
63, (1) pages.
ABSpl   DHU   DLC   NYPLS

BYARS, J.
Black and White. Compiled and Edited by J. C. Byars, Jr. Washington, D. C., The Crane Press, c1927.
96 pages.
HE   HPSpl   NYPLS

(BYER, D. P.)
Conquest of Coomassie. An epic of the Mashanti Nation, by Aldebaran pseud. With illustrations by Henry M. Brooks, Long Branch, California, Worth While Publishing Company, 1926.
103 pages. Portrait.
DLC   HPSpl

CAMPBELL, ALFRED GIBBS.
Poems, by Alfred Gibbs Campbell. Newark, N. J., Advertiser Printing House, 1883.
120 pages.
DLC   NYPLS

CAMPBELL, JAMES EDWIN.
Echoes from the Cabin and Elsewhere, by James Edwin Campbell. Chicago, The Author (Donohu and Hennebery, Printers, 1895.)
86 pages. Portrait.
DHU   DC   DPSpl

CANNON, DAVID WADSWORTH.
Black Labor Chant and Other Poems, by David Wadsworth Cannon, Jr. 1910-1938. New York, The National Council on Religion in Higher Education, 1939.
56 pages. Portrait.
ABSpl   DHU   DLC   HE   HPSpl   NYPLS

CANNON, NOAH CALWELL.
Interesting Hymns. (In The Rock of Wisdom; An Explanation of the Sacred Scriptures, by the Rev. N. C. Cannon, (a Man of Color) To Which are Added Several Interesting Hymns. New York, 1833.)
p. 144. Portrait.
Seventeen "Interesting Hymns" are included in this volume.
ABSpl   DHU   NYPLS

CARMICHAEL, WAVERLEY TURNER.

From the Heart of a Folk. A Book of Songs, by Waverly
Turner Carmichael. Boston, The Cornhill Company, 1918.
60 pages.
ABSpl DHU HE HPSpl NYPLS

CARRIGAN, NETTIE W.

Rhymes and Jingles for the Children's Hour, by Nettie W.
Carrigan. Boston, The Christopher Publishing House, 1940.
57 pages.
DHU DLC HE

CARTER, HERMAN J. C.

The Scottsboro Blues. Nashville, Tenn., The Mahlon Publishing Co., c1933.
32 pages.
DHU SABpl

CASON, P. MARTIN.

Book of Fifty Poems. Our Brave Heroes, by P. Martin Cason. (No imprint).
64 pages.
HPSpl

CENELLES, LES.

Choix de Poesies Indigenes, Et de ces Fruits qu'ien Dien
Prodigue dans nos Bois Heureux, si j'en ai su Faire un
amable choix! A Mercier. Nouvelle Orleans. Imprime par
H. Lauve et Compagnie, 1845.
215 pages.
ABSpl EMCpl

This was reprinted in New York in 1930 in an edition of
Fifty copies with introduction by Edward Larocque Tinker.
HE

CHERIOT, HENRI.

Black Ink, by the author of Variant Verse. Orlando, Florida, Henri Cheriot Publishing Co. (c1917).
44 pages.
DLC NYPLS

CLARK, MAZIE EARHART.

Garden of Memories by Mazie Earhart Clark. Dedicated
to my Friends in memory of my husband Sgt. George J.
Clark. Cincinnati, Ohio, Eaton Publishing Co. (c1932).
66 pages. Portrait.
ABSpl DLC HPSpl

24

CLARK, MAZIE EARHART.
Life's Sunshine and Shadows, by Mazie Earhart Clark. Poems of Sunshine and Shadow, of Sorrow and Cheer, Heart-Throbs Revealing What Memory Holds Dear. Cincinnati, Ohio, Eaton Publishing Company, 1940.
112 pages. Portrait.
DHU   DLC

CLARK, PETER WELLINGTON, ED.
Arrows of Gold; an anthology of Catholic verse from "America's First Catholic College for Colored Youth," edited by Peter Wellington Clark. Xavier University Press, 1941.
85(1) pages.
DHU   DLC   NYPLS   ABSpl

CLEM, CHARLES DOUGLASS.
A Little Souvenir. (No imprint, 1908).
8 pages. Portrait.
NYPLS

CLEM, CHARLES DOUGLASS.
Rhyme of a Rhymester. Edmond, Oklahoma, The Author, 1901.
52 pages.
ABSpl   NYPLS

CLIFFORD, CARRIE WILLIAMS.
Race Rhymes. Washington, D. C. Pendleton, 1911.
28 pages. Portrait.
NYPLS

CLIFFORD, CARRIE WILLIAMS.
The Widening Light. Boston, Walter Reid Company (c1922).
65 pages.
DHU   NYPLS

COFFIN, FRANK BARBOUR.
Coffin's Poem and Ajax Ordeals, by F. B. Coffin. Little Rock, Arkansas. The Colored Advocate Printers, n.d.
248 pages. Portrait.
DLC   NYPLS

COLLINS, HARRY JONES.
From Shadow to Sunshine. Cleveland, Ohio, H. J. Collins, 10528 Hudson Ave., 1918.
47 pages.
DHU

COLLINS, LESLIE M.
Exile, A Book of Verse, by Leslie M. Collins. (Atlanta, Ga., The B. F. Logan Press) 1938.
39 pages.
ABSpl

25

COOPER, ANNA JULIA.
Christmas Bells, A One Act Play for Children. (In verse).
(No imprint).
15 pages.

CORBETT, MAURICE N.
The Harp of Ethiopia, by Maurice N. Corbett. Nashville,
Tenn., National Baptist Publishing Board, 1914.
276 pages. Portrait.
ABSpl   DHU   HE   NYPLS

COTTER, JOSEPH SEAMON, JR.
The Band of Gideon and Other Lyrics, by Joseph Seamon
Cotter, Jr. Boston, The Cornhill Company (c1918).
29 pages.
ABSpl   DHU   DLC   HE   HPSpl   NYPLS

COTTER, JOSEPH SEAMON, SR.
Caleb, the Degenerate. A Play in Four Acts. A Study of
Types, Customs and Needs of the American Negro, by
Joseph S. Cotter. Louisville, Kentucky, The Bradley and
Gilbert Company, 1903.
57 pages. Portrait.
ABSpl   DLC   HPSpl   NYPLS   SABpl

COTTER, JOSEPH SEAMON, SR.
Caleb, the Degenerate; a Play in Four Acts. A Study of
the Types, Customs and Needs of the American Negro.
New York, Henry Harrison, c1940.
67 pages.
ABSpl   DHU   HE

COTTER, JOSEPH SEAMON, SR.
Collected Poems of Joseph S. Cotter, Sr. New York, Henry
Harrison, (1938).
78 pages. Portrait.
ABSpl   DHU   DLC   HE   NYPLS

COTTER, JOSEPH SEAMON, SR.
Links of Friendship, by Joseph S. Cotter, Sr. (Four lines of
verse). Louisville, Ky., the Bradley and Gilbert Company,
1898.
64 pages. Portrait.
ABSpl   DLC   HPSpl   NYPLS

COTTER, JOSEPH SEAMON, SR.
A Rhyming, by Joseph S. Cotter. Louisville, Ky., The New
South Publishing Company, 1895.
32 pages.
DLC   HE   HPSpl

COTTER, JOSEPH SEAMON, SR.
Sequel to the "Pied Piper of Hamelin" and Other Poems, by Joseph S. Cotter, Sr. New York, Henry Harrison, (c1939).
93 pages. Portrait.
ABSpl DHU DLC HE HPSpl NYPLS SABpl

COTTER, JOSEPH SEAMON, SR.
Verse for Educators. Louisville, Ky. Folder.
(4) pages.
HE HPSpl

COTTER, JOSEPH SEAMON, SR.
A White Song and a Black One. Louisville, Ky., The Bradley and Gilbert Co., 1909.
64 pages. Portrait.
ABSpl DLC HE HPSpl NYPLS

This author has also published some sheet music with lyrics by him.

COWDERY, MAE V.
We Lift Our Voices and Other Poems: Philadelphia, Alpress, 1936.
68 pages. Frontispiece.
ABSpl AU HE HPSpl NYPLS

CULLEN, COUNTEE.
The Ballad of a Brown Girl, and Old Ballad Retold, by Countee Cullen, with illustrations and decorations by Charles Cullen. New York, London, Harper and Borthers, 1927.
(10) 11 pages.
DHU DLC HE HPSpl NYPLS

Also issued in Special Edition of 500 copies.
HE

CULLEN, COUNTEE.
The Black Christ and Other Poems, by Countee Cullen, with decorations by Charles Cullen. New York and London, Harper and Brothers Publishers, 1929.
110 pages.
ABSpl DHU DLC HPSpl NYPLS

CULLEN, COUNTEE, ED.
Caroling Dust, an anthology of verse by Negro Poets, edited by Countee Cullen. New York and London, Harper and Brothers Publishers, 1927.
237(1) pages.
ABSPL DHU DLC HE HPSPL NYPLS

CULLEN, COUNTEE.
Color, by Countee Cullen. New York and London, Harper and Brothers, 1925.
108 pages.
ABSPL DHU DLC HE HPSPL NYPLS

CULLEN, COUNTEE.
Copper Sun, by Countee Cullen, with decorations by Charles Cullen. New York and London, Harper and Brothers Publishers, 1927.
XI, 89 pages.
ABSPL DHU DLC HE NYPLS

CULLEN, COUNTEE.
The Lost Zoo (A Rhyme for the Young, But not too Young) by Christopher Cat and Countee Cullen, with illustrations by Charles Sebree. New York and London, Harper and Brothers Publishers, 1940.
72 pages.
ABSPL DHU DLC HPSPL NYPLS

CULLEN, COUNTEE.
The Medea and Some Other Poems, by Countee Cullen. New York and London, Harper and Brothers Publishers, 1935.
97 pages.
ABSPL DHU DLC HE HPSPL NYPLS

CUTHBERT, MARION.
April Grasses, by Marion Cuthbert. New York, the Woman's Press, (c1936).
30 pages.
ABSPL DHU DLC NYPLS

DANDRIDGE, RAYMOND GARFIELD.
Penciled Poems by Ray G. Dandridge. Cincinnati, Ohio, The Author, 824 Chateau Ave., 1917.
51 pages. Portrait.
ABSpl DLC HE HPSpl NYPLS

DANDRIDGE, RAYMOND GARFIELD.
The Poet and Other Poems, by Raymond Garfield Dandridge. Cincinnati, Ohio, (C. Powell and White Printers), 1920.
64 pages.
ABSpl DHU DLC HE

DANDRIDGE, RAYMOND GARFIELD.
Zalka Peetruza and Other Poems, by Raymond Garfield Dandridge. Cincinnati, The McDonald Press, 1928.
107 pages. Portrait.
ABSpl DHU HE HPSpl NYPLS AU

DANGERFIELD, ABNER WALKER.
Musings. Washington, D. C., Triangle Printing Company, 1914.
39 pages. Portrait.
HPSpl   NYPLS

DAVIS, DANIEL WEBSTER.
Idle Moments; Containing Emancipation and Other Poems, by D. Webster Davis, with an introduction by John H. Smythe. Baltimore, Md., The Educator of Morgan College, 1895.
81 pages. Portrait.
ABSpl   DLC   NYPLS

DAVIS, DANIEL WEBSTER.
'Weh Down Souf and Other Poems, (by) Daniel Webster Davis, illustrations (by) William L. Sheppard. Cleveland, The Helman-Taylor Company, 1897.
136 pages.
ABSpl   DHU   DLC   HE   HPSpl   NYPLS

DAVIS, ·FRANK MARSHALL.
Black Man's Verse, by Frank Marshall Davis. Chicago, Illinois, The Black Cat Press, 1935.
83 pages.
ABSpl   DHU   DLC   HPSpl   NYPLS

DAVIS, FRANK MARSHALL.
I am the American Negro, by Frank Marshall Davis. Chicago, Illinois, The Black Cat Press, 1937.
66 pages.
ABSpl   DHU   DLC   NYPLS

DAVIS, FRANK MARSHALL.
Through Sepia Eyes, by Frank Marshall Davis. Decorations by William Fleming. Chicago, Illinois, The Black Cat Press, 1938.
10 pages.
ABSpl   DHU   HE   NYPLS

DEAS, KATHERINE.
Life Line Poems, by Mrs. Katherine Deas _____ Chicago, Ill., Published by Edward C. Deas, n.d.
32 pages. Portrait.
HPS

DICKERSON, NOY JASPER.
A Scrap Book, by Noy Jasper Dickerson. Boston, The Christopher Publishing House (c1931).
48 pages.
ABSpl

DINKINS, CHARLES R(OUNTREE).
Lyrics of Love, Sacred and Secular, by Charles R. Dinkins. Columbia, S. C., The State Company, 1904.
230 pages. Portrait.
ABSpl DHU DLC NYPLS

DISMOND, BINGA.
He Who Would Die and Other Poems, Including Haitian Vignettes. New York, Wendell Malliett and Co., 1943.
92 pages.
ABSpl DHU HE HPSpl

DUNBAR, PAUL LAURENCE.
Candle-Lightin' Time, by Paul Laurence Dunbar, illustrated with photographs by the Hampton Institute Camera Club and decorations by Margaret Armstrong. New York, Dodd, Mead and Co., 1901.
127 pages.
ABSpl DHU DLC HE HPSpl NYPLS

DUNBAR, PAUL LAURENCE.
Candle-Lightin' Time, by Paul Laurence Dunbar, illustrated with photographs by Margaret Armstrong. New York, Dodd, Mead and Company, 1908.
127 pages.
ABSpl DHU

DUNBAR, PAUL LAURENCE.
Chris' mus' is a' comin' and Other Poems. New York, Dodd, Mead and Company (1905).
48 pages.
HE

Also: Special Christmas gift edition, N. Y. 1907.
48 pages.
ABSpl

DUNBAR, PAUL LAURENCE.
The Complete Poems of Paul Laurence Dunbar, with an Introduction to "Lyrics of Lowly Life," by W. D. Howells. New York, Dodd, Mead and Co., 1910.
289 pages. Portrait.
DLC

DUNBAR, PAUL LAURENCE.
The Complete Poems of Paul Laurence Dunbar, with an introduction to "Lyrics of Lowly Life," by W. D. Howells. New York, Dodd, Mead and Co., 1913.
289 pages. Portrait.
DHU DLC HPSpl

DUNBAR, PAUL LAURENCE.
  The Complete Poems of Paul Laurence Dunbar. With the
  Introduction to "Lyrics of Lowly Life," by W. D. Howells.
  New York, Dodd, Mead and Company, 1921.
  289 pages. Portrait.
  ABSpl NYPLS

DUNBAR, PAUL LAURENCE.
  The Complete Poems of Paul Laurence Dunbar, with an
  Introduction to "Lyrics of Lowly Liife," by W. D. Howells.
  New York, Dodd, Mead and Co., 1926.
  289 pages. Portrait.
  HPSPL
  Also: New York, 1930.
  HE

DUNBAR, PAUL LAURENCE.
  The Complete Poems of Paul Laurence Dunbar, with the
  introduction "Lyrics of Lowly Life," by W. D. Howell. New
  York, Dodd, Mead and Company, 1940.
  289 pages. Portrait.
  DLC

DUNBAR, PAUL LAURENCE.
  Dream Lovers; An Operatic Romance, by Paul Laurence
  Dunbar and S. Coleridge Taylor. London and New York,
  Boosey and Company, 1898.
  37 pages. (Musical score by Samuel Coleridge Taylor).
  DHU

DUNBAR, PAUL LAURENCE.
  The Heart of Happy Hollow, by Paul Laurence Dunbar,
  illustrated by E. W. Kemble. New York, Dodd, Mead and
  Company, 1904.
  309 pages.
  ABSpl DLC NYPLS

DUNBAR, PAUL LAURENCE.
  The Heart of Happy Hollow, by Paul Lawrence Dunbar, il-
  lustrated by E. W. Kemble. New York, Dodd, Mead and
  Company, 1905.
  309 pages.
  DLC

DUNBAR, PAUL LAURENCE.
  Howdy Honey Howdy, by Paul Laurence Dunbar. Illustrated with Photographs by Leigh Richmond Miner. Decorations by Will Jenkins. New York, Dodd, Mead and Company, 1905.
  125 unnumbered pages.
  ABSpl DHU DLC HE HPSpl NYPLS

DUNBAR, PAUL LAURENCE.
Joggin' Erlong, by Paul Laurence Dunbar, illustrated with photographs by Leigh Richmond Miner and decorations by John Rae. New York, Dodd, Mead and Company, 1906. 119 pages.
ABSpl DHU DLC HE DPSpl NYPLS

DUNBAR, PAUL LAURENCE.
The Life and Works of Paul Laurence Dunbar. .... With an Introduction by William Dean Howells, Naperville, Illinois, Published by J. L. Nichols and Co., 1896.
430 pages. Portrait.
HPSpl

DUNBAR, PAUL LAURENCE.
The Life and Works of Paul Laurence Dunbar, containing his Complete Poetical Works, his Best Short stories, numerous Anecdotes and a complete Biography of the famous poet, by Lida Keck Wiggins, and an introduction by William Dean Howells .... profusely illustrated with one half a hundred full page photographs and half-tone engravings. Napervile, Illinois, J. L. Nicols and Company, (c1907). 430 pages.
ABSpl DHU DLC HPSpl NYPLS

DUNBAR, PAUL LAURENCE.
Li'l Gal, by Paul Laurence Dunbar, illustrated with photographs by Leigh Richmond Miner and decorations by Margaret Armstrong. New York, Dodd, Meade and Company, 1904.
ABSpl DHU DLC HE HPSpl NYPLS

DUNBAR, PAUL LAURENCE.
Little Brown Baby, (by) Paul Laurence Dunbar. Poems for Young People. Selections, with Biographical Sketch by Bertha Rodgers. New York, Dodd, Mead and Company, 1940.
106 pages. (Twenty-five poems reprinted).
ABSpl DHU DLC NYPLS

DUNBAR, PAUL LAURENCE.
Lyrics of Love and Laughter, by Paul Laurence Dunbar. New York, Dodd, Mead and Company, 1903.
180 pages.
ABSplDHU DLC HE HPSpl NYPLS

DUNBAR, PAUL LAURENCE.
Lyrics of Lowly Life, by Paul Laurence Dunbar, with an introduction by W. D. Howells. New York, Dodd, Meade and Company, 1896.
208 pages.
ABSpl DHU DLC HE NYPLS

DUNBAR, PAUL LAURENCE.
Lyrics of Lowly Life; with an Introduction by W. D. Howells.
New York, Young People's Missionary Movement of the
United States and Canada (1896).
208 pages.
NYPLS

DUNBAR, PAUL LAURENCE.
Lyrics of Lowly Life, by Paul Laurence Dunbar, with an
introduction by W. D. Howells. New York, Dodd, Meade
and Company, 1897.
208 pages.
DHU   HE

DUNBAR, PAUL LAURENCE.
Lyrics of Lowly Life; with an Introduction by W. D. Howells.
London, Chapman & Hall, Ltd., 1897.
208 pages. Portrait.
NYPLS

DUNBAR, PAUL LAURENCE.
Lyrics of Lowly Life by Paul Laurence Dunbar, with an in-
troduction by W. D. Howells. New York, Dodd, Mead &
Co., 1899.
20, 208 pages. Portrait.
HE   HPSpl
Also: New York, 1902.
HE

DUNBAR, PAUL LAURENCE.
Lyrics of Lowly Life, by Paul Laurence Dunbar, with an in-
troduction by W. D. Howells. New York, Dodd, Meade &
Co., 1908.
208 pages. Portrait.
HPSpl
Also: New York, 1909.
HE

DUNBAR, PAUL LAURENCE.
Lyrics of Lowly Life, by Paul Laurence Dunbar. New York,
Dodd, Mead and Company, 1928.
208 pages. Portrait.
DHU

DUNBAR, PAUL LAURENCE.
Lyrics of Sunshine and Shadow, by Paul Laurence Dun-
bar. New York, Dodd, Mead & Company, 1905.
109 pages.
DLC   NYPLS
Also: New York, 1909.
HE

DUNBAR, PAUL LAURENCE.
Lyrics of Sunshine and Shadow, by Paul Laurence Dunbar.
New York, Dodd, Meade & Co., 1914.
109 pages.
HPS   ABSpl

DUNBAR, PAUL LAURENCE.
Lyrics of the Hearthside, by Paul Laurence Dunbar. New
York, Dodd, Mead and Company, 1899.
227 pages. Portrait.
ABSpl   DHU   DLC   HE   HPSpl   NYPLS

DUNBAR, PAUL LAURENCE.
Lyrics of the Hearthside, by Paul Laurence Dunbar. New
York, Dodd, Mead and Company, 1901.
227 pages. Portrait.
DHU

DUNBAR, PAUL LAURENCE.
Lyrics of the Hearthside. New York, Dodd, Mead and Company, 1908.
227 pages. Portrait.
DHU

DUNBAR, PAUL LAURENCE.
Majors and Minors: Poems, by Paul Laurence Dunbar.
Toledo, Ohio, Hadley and Hadley, Printers and Binders,
1895.
148 pages. Portrait.
ABSpl   DHU   HE   HPSpl   NYPLS

DUNBAR, PAUL LAURENCE.
Oak and Ivy by Paul Laurence Dunbar. Dayton, Ohio,
Press of United Brethren Publishing House, 1893.
62 pages.
ABSpl   HE   HPSpl   NYPLS
Work, p. 458, is in error listing 1892 edition.

DUNBAR, PAUL LAURENCE.
Poems of Cabin and Field. Illustrated with photographs by
the Hampton Institute Camera Club and decorations by
Alice Morse. New York, Dodd, Mead and Company, 1899.
125 pages.
DHU   DLC   HE   NYPLS
Also: New York, 1900.
HE

DUNBAR, PAUL LAURENCE.
Poems of Cabin and Field; Illustrated with photographs by
the Hampton Institute Camera Club and Decorations by
Alice Morse. New York, Dodd, Mead & Co., 1904.
125 pages.
NYPLS

DUNBAR, PAUL LAURENCE.
Poems of Cabin and Field, by Paul Laurence Dunbar. New York, Dodd, Mead & Co., 1908.
125 pages.
DHU   HPSpl

DUNBAR, PAUL LAURENCE.
Speakin' o' Christmas and Other Christmas and Special Poems. New York, Dodd, Mead and Company, 1914.
96 pages.
ABSpl   DHU   DLC   HE   NYPLS

DUNBAR, PAUL LAURENCE.
When Malindy Sings, by Paul Laurence Dunbar, illustrated with photographs by the Hampton Institute Camera Club, decoration by Margaret Armstrong. New York, Dodd, Mead and Company, 1903.
144 pages. Portrait.
ABSpl   DLC   HE   NYPLS

Also: New York, 1904.
HE

DUNBAR, PAUL LAURENCE.
When Malindy sings, by Paul Laurence Dunbar, illustrated with photographs by the Hampton Institute Camera Club. Decoration by Margaret Armstrong. New York, Dodd, Mead and Co., 1906.
144 pages. Portrait.
HPSpl

DUNGEE, JOHN RILEY.
Random Rhymes, Formal and Dialect, Sermons and Humorous Racial, Religious, Patriotic and Sentimental, by J. Riley Dungee. Norfolk, Va., Guide Publishing Co., Inc. 1929.
101, 2 pages. Portrait.
DHU   DLC   NYPLS

EASTMOND, CLAUDE T.
Light and Shadows, by Claude T. Eastmond. Boston, The Christopher Publishing House, (c1934).
66 pages.
ABSpl   DHU

EDWIN, WALTER LEWIS.
"Songs in the Desert." London, Frank H. Morland, 1909.
31 pages.
NYPLS

EPPERSON, ALOISE BARBOUR.
>   The Hills of Yesterday and Other poems. (Washington, D.
>   C., printed by James A. Brown, 1533 Ninth Street, N. W.
>   (1944).
>   74 pages. Portrait.
>   ABSpl   DHU   HE

EXPERIENCES of a Heart. Its Joys, Its Sorrows.   Poems by
>   Anonymous. Boston, Meador Publishing Company, 1931.
>   68 pages.
>   ABSpl

FIELDS, MAURICE C.
>   The Collected Poems of Maurice C. Fields. New York, The
>   Exposition Press (c1940).
>   64 pages.
>   DHU   DLC   NYPLS

FIELDS, MAURICE.
>   Testament of Youth. New York, Pegasus Publishing Com-
>   pany, (c1941).
>   32 pages.
>   DLC   NYPLS

FIGGS, CARRIE LAW MORGAN.
>   Nuggets of Gold, by Carrie Law Morgan Figgs. Chicago,
>   Ill., c1921.
>   31 pages.
>   ABSpl

FIGGS, CARRIE LAW MORGAN.
>   Poetic Pearls, by Carrie Law Morgan Figgs. Jacksonville,
>   Florida, Edward Waters College Press, 1920.
>   32 pages. Portrait.
>   ABSpl

FISHER, GERTRUDE ARQUENE.
>   Original Poems, by Gertrude Arquene Fisher. Parsons,
>   Kansas, Foley Railway Printing Company, (c1910).
>   11 pages. Portrait.
>   ABSpl

FLANAGAN, THOMAS JEFFERSON.
>   By the Pine Knot Torches. Atlanta, Ga., The Dickcut Co.,
>   (c1921).
>   64 pages. Portrait.
>   AU   HE

FLANNAGAN, THOMAS JEFFERSON.
>   The Canyons at Providence. (The Lay of the Clay Min-
>   strel). Atlanta, Ga., The Author, 1941.
>   21 pages.
>   ABSpl

FLANNAGAN, THOMAS JEFFERSON.
The Harvest Hymn. Atlanta, Ga., Privately Printed (n.d.)
12 pages. Portrait.
AU

FLANAGAN, THOMAS JEFFERSON.
The Road to Mount McKeithan. Atlanta, Ga., Independent
Publishers Corporation, 1927.
38 & 12 pages. Portrait.
AU ABSpl

FLANAGAN, THOMAS JEFFERSON.
Smilin' thru the Corn, and Other Verse. Atlanta, Ga., Independent Publishers Corporation (c1927).
63 pages.
AU ABSpl

FLEMING, SARAH LEE BROWN.
Clouds and Sunshine, by Sarah Lee Brown Fleming. Boston, The Cornhill Company (c1920).
53 pages.
ABSpl HPSpl DLC

FORD, NICK AARON.
Songs from the Dark, by Nick Aaron Ford. Boston, Meador
Publishing Company, 1940.
40 pages.
ABSpl DLC HE HPSpl

FORD, ROBERT EDGAR.
Brown Chapel, a Story in Verse by Rev. Robert E. Ford.
(Baltimore?) 1905.
307 pages. Portrait.
ABSpl HPSpl DLC NYPLS

FORDHAM, MARY WESTON.
Magnolia Leaves. Poems by Mary Weston Fordham, with
an introduction by Booker T. Washington, Prin.. Tuskegee
Institute. Tuskegee, Ala. (Charleston, S. C., Walker, Evans.
and Cogswell Co., 1897).
104 pages.
DHU HE NYPLS

FORTSON, BETTIOLA HELOISE.
(Mental Pearls). Original Poems and Essays. (Chicago, Illinois). 1915.
66 pages. Portrait.
ABSpl DHU

FORTUNE, MICHAEL.
New Year's Anthem as Sung in the African Episcopal Church of St. Thomas. Jan. 1, 1808.
In Jones, Absalom. A Thanksgiving Sermon Preached January 1, 1808, in St. Thomas', or the African Episcopal Church, Philadelphia. Philadelphia: Printed for the use of the Congregation. Fry and Kammerer, Printer, 1808.
(23)-24 pages.
NYHS NYPL

FORTUNE, TIMOTHY THOMAS.
Dreams of Life. Miscellaneous Poems, by Timothy Thomas Fortune and Peterson, Publishers, 1905.
192 pages. Portrait.
DHU HE HPSpl NYPLS

FOUR LINCOLN UNIVERSITY POETS. Foreword by President William Hallock Johnson. Waring Cuney, William Alleyn Hill, Edward Silvera, and Langston Hughes. Lincoln University Herald. v. 33, No. 3, March 1930.
16 pages.
ABSpl DHU

FRANKLIN, JAMES T(HOMAS).
Mid-Day Gleaning, a book of home and holiday reading, by James T. Franklin. Memphis, Tenn., Tracy Printing and Stationery Co., 1893.
1943 pages. Portrait. (Verse and Prose).
DLC NYPLS

FULTON, DAVID BRYANT.
Mother of Mine. Ode to the Negro Woman, by David B. Fulton. (Four lines of verse from Solomon's Song. 643). New York, August Valentine Bernier, Printer, 79 W. 131st Street, c1923.
10 pages. Portrait.
DLC HPSpl

FULTON, DAVID BRYANT.
Poem, Abraham Lincoln by "Jack Thorne" (pseud.). Written at the request of the Colored Citizens' Lincoln Centenary Committee, and read before two thousand five hundred people at the Baptist Temple, (Brooklyn, New York, February 12th, 1909).
5, 1 pages. Portrait.
DHU DLC NYPLS

GAIRY, RICHARDSON A.
The Poets Vision and The Noblest Struggle; Poems. New York, New York Age Publishing Co., (1909).
38 pages.
NYPLS

GARDNER, BENJAMIN FRANKLIN.
    Black, by Benjamin Franklin Gardner. Caldwell, Idaho,
    the Caxton Printers, Ltd., 1933.
    79 pages.
    ABSpl DHU DLC HE NYPLS

GARVEY, MARCUS.
    Selections from the Poetic Meditations of Marcus Garvey.
    New York, Published by Amy Jacques Garvey (c1927).
    30 pages.
    ABSpl

GARVEY, MARCUS.
    The Tragedy of White Injustice, by Marcus Garvey. (New
    York, Published by Amy Jacques Garvey. 133 W. 129th
    Street. c1927).
    22 pages.
    HPSpl

GHOLSON, EDWARD.
    Musings of a Minister, by Rev. Edward Gholson. Boston,
    The Christopher Publishing House, (c1943).
    101 pages.
    HPSpl DLC

GIBSON, POWELL W.
    Grave and Comic Rhymes, by P. W. Gibson. Alexandria,
    Va., Murray Bros., Printers, 1904.
    (46) pages. Portrait.
    DHU

GILBERT, MERCEDES.
    Selected Gems of Poetry, Comedy and Drama, by Mercedes
    Gilbert. Boston, The Christopher Publishing House. (c1931).
    89 pages. First 39 pages or poetry.
    ABSpl DLC HE HPSpl NYPLS

GILL, CLEMENT C.
    Poems. Washington, D. C., Howard University, 1904-1905.
    Broadside.
    DHU

GILMORE, F. GRANT.
    Masonic and Other Poems. (The Author, n.p., c1908).
    20 pages. Portrait.
    ABSpl HPSpl NYPLS

GOODWIN, RUBY BERKLEY.
    From My Kitchen Window. The Poems of Ruby Berkley
    Goodwin. With an Introduction by Margaret Widdemer.
    New York, Wendell Malliet and Company, 1942.
    66 pages.
    ABSpl HPSpl NYPLS

GORDON, SELMA.
Poems, by Selma Gordon. Book No. 4. (No imprint).
19 pages.
ABSpl

GORDON, SELMA.
Special Poems, by Selma Gordon. (No imprint).
19 pages.
ABSpl

GRAVES, LINWOOD D.
"It's the Same Old Story." A Tribute to Joe Louis, also "The
True Friend" by Linwood D. Graves. Big Stone Gap, Vir-
ginia, 291 E. 5th Street, 1939.
(4) pages. Portrait.
DHU

GRAVES, LINWOOD D.
Mother, also "The Hidden Flower." The Booklet "Every"
Individual Should Own, by Linwood D. Graves (The Poet
of Simplicity). (No imprint).
ABSpl

GRAVES, LINWOOD D.
Poems of Simplicity and the Living Dead. A Short True
Story, by Linwood D. Graves. Kingsport, Tenn., Kingsport
Press, Inc., 1938.
116 pages. Portrait.
DHU   DLC

GREENER, RICHARD THEODORE.
Christmas Bells. (No imprint). Broadside, 8½x19½cm.
HU

HAMMON, JUPITER.
An Address to Miss Phillis Wheatly (sic) Ethiopian Poetess,
in Boston, who came from Africa at eight years of age, and
soon became acquainted with the Gospel of Jesus Christ.
Composed by Jupiter Hammon, a Negro man belonging
to Mr. Joseph Lloyd, of Queen's Village, on Long-Island,
now in Hartford. Hartford, 1778.
Broadside.
CHS

HAMMON, JUPITER.
A Dialogue Entitled, The Kind Master and the Dutiful Servant. In Hammon, Jupiter. An Evening's Improvement.
Showing, the Necessity of Beholding the Lamb of God. To
Which is added, a Dialogue, Entitled, The Kind Master and
the Dutiful Servant. Written by Jupiter Hammon, a Negro
man belonging to Mr. John Lloyd, of Queen's Village, on

Long Island, now in Hartford. Hartford, Printed for the Author, by the Assistance of His Friends. (c1790?)
(23)-28 pages.
DLC NYHS

HAMMON, JUPITER.
An Evening Thought. Salvation by Christ, with Penetial Cries: Composed by Jupiter Hammon, a Negro belonging to Mr. Lloyd, of Queen's Village on Long-Island, the 25th of December, 1760.
Broadside.
NYHS

HAMMON, JUPITER.
A Poem for Children with Thoughts on Death. In Hammon, Jupiter. A Winter Piece: Being a Serious Exhortation, with A call to the Unconverted, and a Short Contemplation on the Death of Jesus Christ. Written by Jupiter Hammon, a Negro Man belonging to Mr. John Lloyd, of Queen's Village, on Long Island, now in Hartford. Published by the Author with the Assistance of His Friends. Hartford: Printed for the Author, 1782.
(23)-24 pages.
CHS MHS PPL

HANDY, OLIVE LEWIS.
My Deeply Solemn Thoughts, by Olive Lewis Handy. (c1939, by Olive Lewis Handy).
35 pages.
HPSpl

HANDY, W. H.
Truths in Rhyme, and Miscellaneous Prose Compositions by W. H. Handy. Printed in the United States of America for the Author by The Caxton Press. (1928).
66 pages.
HE

HARE, MAUD CUNEY.
The Message of the Trees; An Anthology of Leaves and Branches. With a Foreword by William Stanley Braithwaite. Boston, The Cornhill Publishing Company, (c1918).
190 pages.
ABSpl HPSpl NYPLS

HARLESTON, EDWARD NATHANIEL.
The Toiler's Life; Poems, by Edward Nathaniel Harleston, with an introduction by L. S. Crandell. Philadelphia, The Jenson Press, 1907.
238 pages. Portrait.
ABSpl DHU HPSpl NYPLS

HARPER, FRANCES ELLEN WATKINS.
    The Alabama Martyr and Other Poems. (No imprint).
    24 pages. Portrait.
    HPSpl

HARPER, FRANCES ELLEN WATKINS.
    Atlanta Offering Poems, by Frances E. W. Harper. Phila-
    delphia, The Author, 1006 Bainbridge Street, 1895.
    70 pages. Portrait.
    DHU

HARPER, FRANCES ELLEN WATKINS.
    Idylls of the Bible, by F. E. W. Harper. Philadelphia, The
    Author, 1006 Bainbridge Street, 1901.
    64 pages. Portrait.
    DHU HPSpl

HARPER, FRANCES ELLEN WATKINS.
    Moses. A Story of the Nile, by Mrs. F. E. W. Harper. 2d
    ed. Philadelphia, Merrihew & Son, Printers, 1869.
    47 pages. Portrait.
    Pages 43-47 prose. "The Mission of the Flower."
    NYPLS

HARPER, FRANCES ELLEN WATKINS.
    Moses: A Story of the Nile, 2d ed., by F. E. W. Harper.
    Philadelphia, The Author, 1006 Bainbridge Street, 1889.
    52 pages.
    DHU NYPLS

HARPER, FRANCES ELLEN WATKINS.
    Moses, a Story of the Nile, by Mrs. F. E. W. Harper, 2nd
    edition. Philadelphia, The Author, 1006 Bainbridge Street,
    1893.
    64 pages.
    HPSpl

HARPER, FRANCES ELLEN WATKINS.
    Poems, (by) Frances E. Watkins Harper. Philadelphia, Mer-
    rihew and Son, 1871.
    48 pages.
    DLC

HARPER, FRANCES ELLEN WATKINS.
    Poems, by Frances E. Watkins Harper. Providence, A.
    Crawford Greene & Son. Printers, 1880.
    48 pages.
    ABSpl

HARPER, FRANCES ELLEN WATKINS.
Poems, by Frances E. W. Harper. Philadelphia, 1896.
74 pages.
ABSpl

HARPER, FRANCES ELLEN WATKINS.
Poems, by Frances E. W. Harper. Philadelphia, The Author,
1006 Bainbridge Street, 1898.
74 pages.
ABSpl   DHU   HE   HPSpl

HARPER, FRANCES ELLEN WATKINS.
Poems, by Frances E. Harper. Philadelphia, The Author,
1006 Brainbridge Street, 1900.
90 pages. Portrait.
ABSpl DHU HE NYPLS

HARPER, FRANCES ELLEN WATKINS.
Poems on Miscellaneous Subjects, by Frances Ellen Watkins, 2d ed. Boston, J. B. Yerrington and Sons, Printers, 1854.
40 pages. First 32 pages are poetry.
ABSpl DLC

HARPER, FRANCES ELLEN WATKINS.
Poems on Miscellaneous Subjects, by Frances Ellen Watkins. Tenth Thousand, Philadelphia, Merrihew & Thompson, Printers, 1857.
56 pages.
HPSpl DLC NYPLS

HARPER, FRANCES ELLEN WATKINS.
Poems on Miscellaneous Subjects, by Frances Ellen Wat-
kins Harper. 20th ed. Philadelphia, Merrihew & Son,
Printers, 1871.
56 pages. Prose, p. 47-56.
NYPLS

HARPER, FRANCES ELLEN WATKINS.
Poems on Miscellaneous Subjects, by Frances Ellen Wat-
kins Harper. 20th ed. Philadelphia, Merrihew and Son,
Printers, 1874.
56 pages. Prose, Miscellaneous Writings, pages 48-56.
ABSpl

HARPER, FRANCES ELLEN WATKINS.
Sketches of Southern Life, by Frances E. Watkins Harper.
Philadelphia, Merrihew and Son, Printers, 1872.
24 pages.
NYPLS
Also: Philadelphia, 1873.
HE

HARPER, FRANCES ELLEN WATKINS.
    Sketches of Southern Life, by Frances E. Watkins Harper.
    Philadelphia, Ferguson Bros. & Co., 1887.
    58 pages. Portrait.

    Reissue with new title page with imprint—Philadelphia,
    Merrihew and Son, Printers, 1888.
    ABSpl

HARPER, FRANCES ELLEN WATKINS.
    Sketches of Southern Life, by Frances E. Watkins Harper.
    Philadelphia, Ferguson Bros., and Co., printers, 1888.
    58 pages.
    On cover. Philadelphia, Ferguson Brothers and Co., 1887.
    NYPLS

    Also: Philadelphia, 1890.
    HE

HARPER, E. WATKINS.
    Sketches of Southern Life. By Frances E. Watkins Harper.
    Philadelphia: Ferguson Bros. & Co., Printers, No. 15 North
    Seventh Street. 1891.
    58 pages.
    NYHS

HARPER, FRANCES ELLEN WATKINS.
    Sketches of Southern Life by Frances E. Watkins Harper.
    Philadelphia, Ferguson Bros. & Co., Printers, 1896.
    48 pages.
    HPSpl   NYPLS

HARPER, FRANCES ELLEN WATKINS.
    The Sparrow's Fall and Other Poems, by Frances E. W.
    Harper. (No imprint).
    22 pages. Portrait.
    ABSpl   NYPLS

HARRIS, LEON R.
    The Steel Makers and Other Poems, by Leon R. Harris.
    Portsmouth, Ohio, Published at the T. C. McConnell Print-
    ery, (c1918).
    15 pages. Portrait.
    ABSpl

HARRISON, JAMES M.
    Southern Sunbeams, a Book of Poems, by James M. Harri-
    son. Richmond, Va., The Saint Luke Press, 1926.
    100 pages.
    ABSpl   DHU   HPSpl

HART, ESTELLE PUGSLEY.
Thoughts in Poetry by Estelle P. Hart. New York, Tobias
Press (c1911).
143 pages.
DLC HPSpl NYPLS

HATCHETTE, WILFRED IRWIN.
Youth's Flight. A Collection of Poems. St. Thomas, Virgin
Islands, Art Shop Press, c1938.
38 pages.
ABSpl NYPLS

HAWKINS, WALTER EVERETTE.
Chords and Discords, by Walter Everette Hawkins. Washington, D. C. The Murray Brothers Press, 1909.
81 pages. Portrait.
DHU DLC HPSpl NYPLS

HAWKINS, WALTER EVERETTE.
Chords and Discords, by Walter Everette Hawkins, 2d ed.
Boston, R. G. Badger, c1920.
100 pages.
ABSpl DLC NYPLS

HAYDEN, ROBERT EARL.
Heart-Shape in the Dust; Poems by Robert E. Hayden. Detroit, Michigan, the Falson Press (c1940).
63 pages.
ABSpl DLC HE NYPLS

HAYSON, MAXWELL NICY.
Douglass and Washington. (No imprint). Broadside, 16½x
32cm.
HU

HAYSON, MAXWELL NICY.
Samuel Coleridge-Taylor; An Ode of Welcome. (Washington, D. C.. R. L. Pendleton, 1906).
5 unnumbered leaves.
DHU

HEARD, JOSEPHINE D. (HENDERSON).
Morning Glories by Josephine D. (Henderson) Heard. Phila-
delphia, Penn., March 17, 1890. Lancaster. Pa., Speaker
Print (c1890).
108 pages. Portrait.
ABSpl HPSpl NYPLS

HEARD, JOSEPHINE D. (HENDERSON).
Morning Glories, by Josephine D. (Henderson) Heard. Phila-
delphia, Penna., March 17, 1890-1901. 2d ed. Atlanta, Ga.,
The Franklin Printing and Publishing Co., 1901.
142 pages. Portrait.
DHU HE

HENDERSON, ELLIOTT BLAINE.
  Darky Ditties; Poems, by Elliott B. Henderson. Columbus,
  Ohio, 1915.
  54 pages.
  DHU   HE   NYPLS

HENDERSON, ELLIOTT BLAINE.
  Darky Meditations, Poems composed by Elliott Blaine Henderson. Springfield, Ohio. Published by the Author, 1910.
  68 pages. Portrait.
  DHU

HENDERSON, ELLIOTT BLAINE.
  Humble Folks; Poems composed by Elliott Blaine Henderson. Springfield, Ohio, Published by the author, 1909.
  65 pages. Portrait.
  ABSpl   HE   HPSpl   NYPLS

HENDERSON, ELLIOTT BLAINE.
  Jes Plain Black Fo'ks Poems. Composed by Elliott Blaine
  Henderson. Springfield, Ohio (n.d.).
  51 pages. Portrait.
  ABSpl   NYPLS

HENDERSON, ELLIOTT BLAINE.
  Old Fashioned Black Fo'ks. Poems by Elliott Blaine Henderson. Columbus, Ohio, Published by the Author, 1913.
  54 pages. Portrait.
  ABSpl   HPSpl   NYPLS

HENDERSON, ELLIOTT BLAINE.
  Plantation Echoes. A Collection of Original Negro Dialect
  Poems. by Elliott Blaine Henderson. Columbus, Ohio, Press
  of F. J. Heer, 1904.
  95 pages.
  HE   ABSpl   DHU   DLC   NYPLS

HENDERSON, ELLIOTT BLAINE.
  Plantation Echoes. A Collection of Original Negro Dialect
  Poems, by Elliott Blaine Henderson. Columbus, Ohio, Press
  of F. J. Heer, 1905.
  95 pages.
  ABSpl   HE

HENDERSON, ELLIOTT BLAINE.
  The Soliloquy of Satan and Other Poems, by Elliott Blaine
  Henderson. Springfield, Ohio, the Author. 1907.
  64 pages. Portrait.
  ABSpl   DLC   HE   HPSpl   NYPLS

HENDERSON, ELLIOTT BLAINE.
Uneddeekayted Fo'ks; Poems composed by Elliott Blaine Henderson. (n.p.) Published by the Author, 1911.
61 pages. Portrait.
DLC HPSpl NYPLS

HENDERSON, S. S.
Religious Poetry and Christian Thought, A Book for the Family, for the Children, for Sunday School and Young People's Meetings, a Jewel for Ministers and Christian Workers, by Rev. S. S. Henderson. Newark, N. J., The Author, 154 Frelinghuysen Avenue, (1920).
96 pages. Portrait.
DHU DLC

HENRY, THOMAS MILLARD.
The Optimist, by Thomas Millard Henry, New York, Printed by The Hebbons Press, 184 W. 135th Street, c1928.
49 pages. Portrait.
ABSpl DLC NYPLS

HILL, JOHN CALHOUN.
Piccolo, volume I, (by) John Calhoun Hill. Meridian, Mississippi, Tell Framer, Printer and Stationer (n.d.).
140(2) pages. Portrait.
HPSpl

HILL, JULIOUS C.
A Song of Magnolia, by Julious C. Hill. Boston, Meador Publishing Co., 1937.
88 pages.
ABSpl DLC HE NYPLS

HILL, JULIOUS C.
A Sonner Song, by Julious C. Hill. New York, Empire Books, c1935.
63 pages.
ABSpl NYPLS

HILL, LESLIE PINCKNEY.
Toussaint L'Ouverture, a Dramatic History, by Leslie Pinckney Hill. Boston, The Christopher Publishing House, c1928.
137 pages.
A blank verse drama in five acts.
ABSpl DHU DLC NYPLS HPSpl

HILL, LESLIE PINCKNEY.
Wings of Oppression and Other Poems, by Leslie Pinckney Hill. Boston, Stratford Company, 1921.
124 pages.
ABSpl DHU DLC HE HPSpl NYPLS

HILL, MILDRED MARTIN.
A Traipsin' Heart, by Mildred Martin Hill. New York, Wendell Malliet and Company, 1942.
61 pages.
ABSpl DHU DLC HE NYPLS HPSpl

HOLDER, JAMES ELLIOTT.
Ballad. A Christmas Incident. (No imprint) c1905..
7 pages.
ABSpl

HOLDER, JAMES ELLIOTT.
The Colored Man's Appeal to White Americans, by James Elliott Holder. (Atlantic City, the Author, c1906).
(8) pages. Portrait.
SABpl

HOLDER, JAMES ELLIOTT.
The Negro's Prayer (and) The Negro's Psalm of Life, by James E. Holder. (Atlantic City, the Author, c1907).
(3) pages.
SABpl

HOLLOWAY, JOHN WESLEY.
Bandanas. (No imprint).
119 pages.
ABSpl

HOLLOWAY, JOHN WESLEY.
From the Desert, by John Wesley Holloway. New York, Neale Publishing Company, 1919.
147 pages.
DHU DLC ABSpl

HOLLY, JOSEPH C.
Freedom's Offering, A Collection of Poems, by Joseph C. Holly (six lines of verse). Rochester, Chas. H. McDonnell, 1853.
38(1) pages.
ABSpl

HORTON, GEORGE MOSES.
The Hope of Liberty, containing a number of Poetical Pieces, by George Moses Horton. Raleigh, N. C., Joseph Gales and Son, 1829.
22 pages.
DLC

HORTON, GEORGE MOSES.
The Naked Genius, by George Moses Horton, the Colored Bard of North Carolina. Author of "The Black Poet" a Work Being Now Compiled and Revised by Captain Will H. S.

Banks, 9th Michigan Cavalry Volunteers, and Which Will be Ready for Publication about the 1st of October, 1865. Revised and Compiled (Referring of Course to Naked Genius) by Will H. S. Banks, Captain 9th Michigan Cav. Wm. B. Smtih & Co. Southern Field and Fireside Book Publishing House, Raleigh, N. C., 1865.
160 pages.
BA

HORTON, GEORGE MOSES.
Poems by a Slave. Philadelphia, 1837.
23 pages. Reprint of Hope of Liberty.
DHU   NYPLS

HUGHES, JAMES LANGSTON.
Dear Lovely Death, by Langston Hughes. New York. Privately Printed at the Troutbeck Press, 1931.
8 unnumbered leaves. Portrait.
ABSpl   DHU   DLC   HPSpl   NYPLS

HUGHES, JAMES LANGSTON.
Deux Poemes par Federico Garcia Lorca et Langston Hughes. Les Poetes du Monde Defendent le Peuple Espagnol .... numero Trois—Compose a la main por Nancy Cunard et Pablo Neruda Tout le Produits de la Republicaine. (No imprint).
4 leaves. Song of Spain. Signed Langston Hughes, Jan. 1937.
ABSpl

HUGHES, JAMES LANGSTON.
The Dream Keeper and Other Poems, by Langston Hughes, with illustrations by Helen Sewell. New York, Alfred A. Knopf, 1932.
77 pages.
ABSpl   DHU   HPSpl   NYPLS

Also: New York, 1941.
HE

HUGHES, JAMES LANGSTON.
Fine Clothes to the Jew, by Langston Hughes. New York, Alfred A. Knopf, 1927.
89 pages.
ABSpl   DHU   HE   NYPLS

HUGHES, JAMES LANGSTON.
Freedom's Plow, by Langston Hughes. New York, Musette Publishers (1943).
14 pages.
ABSpl   DHU   HE

HUGHES, JAMES LANGSTON.
Jim Crow's Last Stand, by Langston Hughes. (New York).
Negro Publication Society of America (1943).
30 pages. (Race and Culture Series, No. 2).
ABSpl DHU HE HPSpl

HUGHES, JAMES LANGSTON.
A Negro Mother and Other Dramatic Recitations, by Langston Hughes. Titles—The Colored Soldier Broke, The Black
Clown, The Big Timer and Dark Youth. With Decorations
by Prentiss Taylor. New York City, The Golden Stair Press
(1931).
20 pages. Special edition of seventeen copies bound on
Robins paper. Hand colored.
ABSpl (No. 1).

HUGHES, JAMES LANGSTON.
A Negro Mother and Other Dramatic Recitations, by Langston Hughes. Titles—The Colored Soldier, Broke, The Black
Clown, The Big Timer and Dark Youth. With decorations
by Prentiss Taylor. New York City, The Golden Stair Press,
(1932).
20 pages.
DHU NYPLS ABSpl

HUGHES, JAMES LANGSTON.
A New Song, by Langston Hughes. Introduction by Mich-
ael Gold. New York, Published by International Workers
Order, 1938.
31 pages.
ABSpl DHU HE NYPLS

HUGHES, JAMES LANGSTON.
Scottsboro Limited. Four Poems and a Play in Verse, by
Langston Hughes, with Illustrations by Prentiss Taylor. New
York City, Golden Stair Press, 1932.
10 unnumbered leaves.

Edition of 730 bound, large paper copies printed on Papier
de Rives, signed by the author and artist, with the litho-
graphs printed from the original stones.
ABSpl (No. 6).

HUGHES, LANGSTON.
Scottsboro Limited. Four Poems and a Play in Verse, by
Langston Hughes, with Illustrations by Prentiss Taylor.
New York Ctiy, Golden Stair Press, 1932.
10 unnumbered leaves.
ABSpl DHU HE NYPLS

HUGHES, JAMES LANGSTON.
Shakespeare in Harlem, by Langston Hughes, with drawings by E. McKnight Kauffer. New York, Alfred A. Knopf, 1942.
124 pages.
ABSpl   DHU   HE   HPSpl   NYPLS

HUGHES, JAMES LANGSTON.
The Weary Blues, by Langston Hughes. New York, Alfred A. Knopf, 1926.
109 pages.
ABSpl   DHU   DLC   HE   HPSpl   NYPLS

HUNTER, CHARLOTTE E.
Birds of Paradise, by Charlotte E. Hunter. (Baltimore, Md., Printed by L. Gordon and Son, Inc., 1940).
20 leaves.
ABSpl   DHU   DLC   SABpl

The Immortal Fifteen Being a Brief Pageant Depicting the Introduction of Freemasonry Among Colored Men in North America. Written and Published Under the Auspices of the Most Worshipful Grand Lodge of Free and Accepted Masons of Connecticut (c1915).
26 pages. Part prose.
ABSpl

JACKSON, A. J.
A Vision of Life, and Other Poems, by A. J. Jackson. Hillsborough, O., printed at the Highland News Office, 1869.
52 pages.
ABSpl

JACKSON, LAURA F.
Paradise (Cleveland Park) and Other Poems, by Laura F. Jackson. Washington, D. C., R. L. Pendleton Printer, 1920.
8 unnumbered leaves.
DHU

JAMIESON, ROSCOE C.
Negro Soldiers ("These Truly are the Brave") and Other Poems, by Roscoe C. Jamison, 2d ed. Kansas City, Kansas, Press of the Gray Printing Co., 1918.
(16) pages. Portrait.
ABSpl

JARVIS, J. ANTONIO.
Fruits in Passing. Poems, by J. Antonio Jarvis. St. Thomas, Virgin Islands, Published by the Art Shop. (c1932).
99 pages. Portrait.
NYPLS

JEFFERSON, WILSON JAMES.
    Verses by Wilson Jefferson. Boston, R. G. Badger, 1909.
    32 pages.
    DLC

JENKINS, WELBORN VICTOR.
    Trumpet in the New Moon and Other Poems, by Welborn
    Victor Jenkins; foreword by E. H. Webster. Boston, The
    Peabody Press (c1934).
    62 pages.
    ABSpl   NYPLS   SABpl

JENKINS, WILLIAM H.
    "Blossoms" (Dedicated to my Mother), by William H. Jen-
    kins. (Princess Anne, Md., Princess Anne Academy Press,
    n.d.)
    35 pages.
    ABSpl

JETER, G. TROY.
    The Volka Whispers. (c by G. Troy Jeter). 1936.
    46 pages.
    DHU

JOHNSON, ADOLPHUS.
    The Silver Chord: Poems, by Adolphus Johnson. Philadel-
    phia, Pa. n.d.
    48 pages. Portrait.
    ABSpl   HPSpl

JOHNSON, CHARLES BERTRAM.
    The Mantle of Dunbar and Other Poems. (No imprint).
    32 pages.
    ABSpl

JOHNSON, CHARLES BERTRAM.
    Songs of My People by Charles Bertram Johnson. Boston,
    The Cornhill Company, c1918.
    55 pages.
    DHU   DLC   HE   NYPLS

JOHNSON, FENTON.
    A Little Dreaming, by Fenton Johnson. Chicago, The Peter-
    son Linotyping Company, 1913.
    80 pages.
    ABSpl   DHU   HE   HPSpl   NYPLS

JOHNSON, FENTON.
    Songs of the Soil, by Fenton Johnson. New York, Press of
    Trachlenberg Company, (c1916).
    39 pages.
    ABSpl   DLC   NYPLS

JOHNSON, FENTON.
Visions of the Dusk, by Fenton Johnson. New York, (Press of Trachtenberg Co., c1915).
71 pages. Portrait.
ABSpl DLC HPSpl NYPLS

JOHNSON, FRANK A.
Fireside Poems, by Frank A. Johnson. New York, N. Y., Privately Printed, Standard Printing Co. (c1931).
37 pages. Portrait.
DHU DLC HE NYPLS

JOHNSON, GEORGIA DOUGLASS.
An Autumn Love Cycle, by Georgia Douglass Johnson. New York, Harold Vinal, Ltd. 1928.
70 pages.
ABSpl DHU DLC HPSpl NYPLS

JOHNSON, GEORGIA DOUGLASS.
Bronze: A Book of Verse, by Georgia Douglass Johnson, with an introduction by W. E. B. Dubois. Boston, B. J. Brimmer Company, 1922.
101 pages.
ABSpl DHU HPSpl NYPLS

JOHNSON, GEORGIA DOUGLASS.
The Heart of a Woman and Other Poems, by Georgia Douglass Johnson, with an introduction by William Stanley Braithwaite. Boston, Cornhill Company, 1918.
62 pages.
ABSpl DHU DLC HE HPSpl NYPLS

JOHNSON, HENRY THEODORE.
Wings of Ebony, by H. T. Johnson. Philadelphia, A.M.E. Book Concern, 1904.
51 pages. Portrait.
HPSpl NYPLS

JOHNSON, JAMES WELDON, ED.
The Book of American Negro Poetry. Chosen and Edited with an Essay on the Negro's Creative Genius, by James Weldon Johnson. New York, Harcourt, Brace & Co (c1922).
43, 217 pages.
ABSpl DHU HE NYPLS HPSpl

JOHNSON, JAMES WELDON, ED.
The Book of American Negro Poetry. Chosen and Edited with an Essay on the Negro's Creative Genius, by James Weldon Johnson. New York, Harcourt, Brace & Co., 1931.
300 pages.
ABSpl DHU NYPLS

JOHNSON, JAMES WELDON.
  Fifty Years. A Poem Written by James Weldon Johnson,
  a Graduate of Atlanta University and Published in the
  New York Times, January1, 1913; with an Estimate of its
  Merit and a Sketch of the Author. (Atlanta, Ga.) The At-
  lanta University Press (ca. 1913).
  8(1) pages.
  At head of title: Atlanta University Leaflet No. 27.
  ABSpl

JOHNSON, JAMES WELDON.
  Fifty Years and Other Poems, by James Weldon Johnson.
  With an Introduction (by) Brander Mathews. Boston, The
  Cornhill Company (c1917).
  92 pages. Portrait.
  Special edition of 110 copies printed on Japan vellum.
  ABSpl (No. 34   NYPLS (No. 43)

JOHNSON, JAMES WELDON.
  Fifty Years and Other Poems, by James Weldon Johnson,
  with an introduction by Brander Mathews. Boston, The
  Cornhill Company, (c1917).
  92, 1 pages.
  ABSpl   DHU   HPSpl   NYPLS

JOHNSON, JAMES WELDON.
  God's Trombones. Seven Negro Sermons in Verse, by
  James Weldon Johnson. Drawings by Aaron Douglas. New
  York, The Viking Press, 1927.
  56 pages.
  ABSpl   DHU   HE   HPSpl   NYPLS

JOHNSON, JAMES WELDON.
  God's Trombones. Seven Negro Sermons in Verse, by
  James Weldon Johnson. London, George Allen and Un-
  win, Ltd., 1929.
  58 pages.
  ABSpl   NYPLS

JOHNSON, JAMES WELDON.
  Saint Peter Relates an Incident of the Resurrection Day.
  New York, The Viking Press, 1930.
  14 pages.
  Special gift edition of 200 copies.
  ABSpl (No. 11)   SBpl (No. 107)

JOHNSON, JAMES WELDON.
  Saint Peter Relates an Incident. Selected Poems, by James
  Weldon Johnson. New York, The Viking Press, 1935.
  105 pages.
  ABSpl   DHU   HPSpl   NYPLS

JOHNSON, JAMES WELDON.
Die Schopfung (The Creation) Eine Neger Predigt fur eine Singstimme und Acht Instrumente von Louis Guenberg, op. 23. Dichtung von James Weldon Johnson. Wien, Universal-Edition, A. G. 1926.
83 pages.
"Negro sermon for voice and eight instruments."
ABSpl

JOHNSON, JESSIE DAVIS.
Christmas Poems. Washington, D. C., 1213 Que St., 1937.
12 pages. Portrait.
DHU

JOHNSON, MAGGIE POGUE.
Thoughts for Idle Hours. (Roanoke, Va., The Stone Printing and Mfg. Co., c1915).
55(1) pages.
DLC

JOHNSON, MAGGIE POGUE.
Virginia Dreams. Lyrics for the Idle Hour, Tales of the Time Told in Rhyme. (n.p.) c. by John M. Leonard, 1910.
64 pages. Portrait.
SABpl NYPLS

JONES, EDWARD SMYTH.
The Rose that Bloometh in My Heart and Other Poems, by Invincible Ned (pseud). (Louisville?, Ky., c1908).
53 pages. Portrait.
DLC

JONES, EDWARD SMYTH.
Souvenir Poem. Our Greater Louisville. (Louisville, Ky., c1908).
(8) pages.
DLC

JONES, EDWARD SMYTH.
The Sylvan Cabin. A Centenary Ode on the Birth of Lincoln and Other Verse, by Edward Smyth Jones, with an introduction by William Stanley Braithwaite. Boston, Sherman, French and Company, 1911.
96 pages.
DHU HE NYPLS

JONES, EDWARD SMYTH.
The Sylvan Cabin; A Centenary Ode on the Birth of Lincoln; With an Introduction Taken from the New York Times. San Francisco, Published by the Author (c1915).
"Panama-Pacific International Exposition Edition."
ABSpl NYPLS

JONES, EDWARD SMYTH.
The Sylvan Cabin. A Centenary Ode on the Birth of Lincoln, by Edward Smyth Jones, with an introduction taken from the New York Times. Chicago, Published by The Edward Smyth Jones Publishing Company, 1922.
9 unnumbered leaves. Portrait.
DHU

JONES, HAROLD R.
Broadway and Other Poems. (No imprint).
59 pages.
ABSpl

JONES, JOSHUA HENRY.
The Heart of the World, by Joshua Henry Jones. Boston, Stratford Company, c1919.
83 pages.
HE   NYPLS   SABpl

JONES, JOSHUA HENRY.
Poems of the Four Seas, by Joshua Henry Jones. Boston, The Cornhill Company, (c1921).
52 pages.
HE   HPSpl

KING, JEFFERSON.
Darky Philosophy Told in Rhyme. Chicago, Smith Jubilee Music Co., 1906.
61 pages. ·

KIRTON, ST. CLAIR.
Poetic creations, by St. Clair Kirton. Boston, Mass., (1943). Lester Benn, Printer.
36 pages.
DHU

KNOX, JACQUELINE LLOYD.
Bittersweets, A Book of Verse, by Jacqueline Lloyd Knox. (Philadelphia) Dorrance Co., Inc. (c1938).
50 pages.
ABSpl

KNOX, JEAN LINDSAY.
A Key to Brotherhood, by Jean Lindsay Knox, New York, The Paebar Publishing Co., 1932.
12 unnumbered leaves.
DHU

LAINE, HENRY ALLEN.
Foot Prints, by Henry Allen Laine. Richmond, Ky., Cut Rate Printing Co., (c1914).
54 pages. Portrait.
DLC   HE

LAINE, HENRY ALLEN.
Foot Prints. Richmond, Ky., Daily Register Press (1924).
80 pages. Portrait.
NYPLS

LAMBERT, CALVIN STOLLMEYER.
Poems of a West Indian. London, "Poetry of Today." 1938.
35 pages.
NYPLS

LAMBERT, CALVIN STOLLMEYER.
Selected Poems of a West Indian. London, The Fortune
Press, (1940).
58 pages.
NYPLS

LATIMER, LEWIS HOWARD.
Poems of Love and Life, by Lewis Howard Latimer. Dedicated to Mary Wilson Latimer (no imprint). Published by
his Friends and Admirers on the Occasion of His Seventy-
Seventh Birthday, September Fourth, 1925.
xxii pages. Portrait laid in.
NYPLS

LAVIAUX, LEON.
The Ebon Muse, and Other Poems, by Leon Laviaux; Eng-
lished by John Myers O'Hara. Portland, Maine, Smith and
Sale. 1914.
51(1) pages.
DHU   DLC   HE   NYPLS

LEE, JOHN FRANCIS.
Poems. Norfolk, (Va.) Burk and Gregory Print. 1905.
54 pages. Portrait.
DLC

LEE, J(OHN) FRANCIS.
The Prince in Ebony, by J. Francis Lee. (No imprint, c1907).
112 pages.
DHU

LEVY, FERDINAND.
Flashes from the Dark, by Ferdinand Levy. With a sketch
of the author by Louis Le Broquy. Dublin, Printed at the
Sign of the Three Candles, 1941.
45 pages. Portrait.
ABSpl   HE

LINDEN, MRS. CHARLOTTE E.
Autobiography and Poems by Mrs. Henry Linden. (3d ed.)
Springfield, O. (1907?).
64 pages. (Cover-title. Scraps of Time).
DHU   DLC

LINDEN, CHARLOTTE E.
Scraps of Time; Poems, by Mrs. Henry Linden. Springfield, Ohio, The Author, n.d.
16 pages. Portrait.
DHU NYPLS

LOCKE, ALAIN, ED.
Four Negro poets. New York, Simon and Schuster, (c1927).
30 pages. (The Pamphlet Poets Series).
NYPLS HE SABpl

LOVE, ROSE LEARY.
Nebraska and His Granny, by Rose Leary Love, with illustrations by Preston Haygood. Tuskegee, Ala., Tuskegee Institute Press, 1936.
69 pages.
ABSpl DLC

LYNCH, CHARLES.
Gladys Klyne and More Harmony. Boston, The Gotham
Press, 1915.
75 pages.
NYPLS

LYNN, EVE.
No Alabaster Box and Other Poems, by Eve Lynn. With
an introduction by Gene Rhodes. Philadelphia, Alpress,
1936.
37 pages. Edition of 350 copies.
ABSpl (Copy No. 264).

McBROWN, GERTRUDE PARTHENIA.
The Picture-Poetry Book, by Gertrude Parthenia McBrown.
Illustrations by Lois Mailou Jones. Washington, D. C., The
Associated Publishers, Inc., 1935.
73 pages.
ABSpl DHU HE HPSpl NYPLS

McCLELLAN, GEORGE MARION.
The Path of Dreams, by George Marion McClellan. Louisville, Ky., John P. Morton and Company (c1916).
76 pages.
ABSpl DHU HE NYPLS

McCLELLAN, GEORGE MARION.
Poems, by George Marion McClellan. Nashville, Tenn.,
Publishing House A.M.E. Church, Sunday School Union,
1895.
145 pages.
95 pages of poetry, 50 pages of prose.
DHU HE HPLpl

McCLELLAN, GEORGE MARION.
Songs of a Southerner. Boston, Press of Rockwell and Churchill, 1896.
16 pages. Portrait.
ABSpl

McCORKLE, GEORGE WASHINGTON.
Poems of Thought and Cheer, by George Washington McCorkle. Petersburg, Va. (No imprint).
16 pages.
ABSpl

McCORKLE, GEORGE WASHINGTON.
Poems of Thought and Cheer, (by) George Washington McCorkle. Washington, D. C., Published under the auspices of the National Bureau of Negro Writers and Entertainers, 1325 Corcoran Street, N. W., n.d.
21 pages.
ABSpl   HPSpl

McDONALD, SAMUEL E.
The Other Girl with Some Further Stories and Poems, by Samuel E. McDonald. New York, Broadway Publishing Company, 1903.
80 pages. (Poetry pages 66-80).
DLC   HPSpl

McGEE, PERRY HONCE.
My Valued Ruby; Poems, by Perry Honce McGee. Washington, Pa. (The Author, Box 314), c1920.
90 pages. Portrait.
DLC

McGIRT, JAMES EPHRAIM.
Avenging the Maine, A Drunken A. B., and Other Poems, by James Ephraim McGirt. Raleigh, Edwards and Broughton, Printers and Binders, 1899.
86 pages. Portrait.
DHU

McGIRT, JAMES EPHRAIM.
Avenging the Maine, a Drunken A. B., and other poems, by James Ephraim McGirt. 2d enl. ed. Raleigh, Edwards and Broughton, Printers and Binders, 1900.
109 pages. Portrait.
HPSpl   NYPLS

McGIRT, JAMES EPHRAIM.
Avenging the Maine, a Drunken A.B. and Other Poems, by James Ephraim McGirt, 3d rev. and enl. ed. Philadelphia, George F. Lasher, Printer and Binder. 1901.
119 pages. Portrait.
HE   HPSpl   NYPLS

McGIRT, JAMES EPHRAIM.
For Your Sweet Sake; poems, by James E. McGirt. Philadelphia, The John C. Winston Co. (c1906).
79 pages. Portrait.
AU   DHU   HE   HPSpl   NYPLS

McGIRT, JAMES EPHRAIM.
Some Simple Songs and a Few More Abmitious Attempts,
(by) James E. McGirt. Philadelphia, Pa., George F. Lasher,
Printer and Binder, 1901.
72 pages. Portrait.
AU   HPDpl   NYPLS

McKAY, CLAUDE.
Constab Ballads, by Claude McKay. London, Watts and
Company, 1912.
94 pages.
ABSpl   DHU   NYPLS

McKAY, CLAUDE.
Harlem Shadows. The Poems of Claude McKay with an
introduction by Max Eastman. New York, Harcourt, Brace
and Company, (c1922).
95 pages.
ABSpl   DHU   HPSpl   NYPLS

McKAY, CLAUDE.
Songs from Jamaica. London, Augener, Ltd., (c1912).
11 pages. Six verses set to music.
ABSpl   DHU

McKAY, CLAUDE.
Songs of Jamaica, by Claude McKay, with an introduction
by Walter Jekyll. Kinigston, Jamaica, Aston W. Gardner
and Co., 1912.
140 pages. Portrait.
ABSpl   DHU   NYPLS

McKAY, CLAUDE.
Spring in New Hampshire, and Other Poems, by Claude
McKay. London, Grant Richards, Ltd., 1920.
40 pages. Portrait.
ABSpl   DHU   HPSpl   NYPLS

MARGETSON, GEORGE REGINALD.
England in the West Indies; A Neglected and Degenerat-
ing Empire. Cambridge, Mass., George Reginald Margetson, c1906.
35 pages.
ABSpl   HBSpl   NYPLS

60

MARGETSON, GEORGE REGINALD.
Ethiopia's Flight. The Negro Question; or, The White Man's
Fear, by George Reginald Margetson. Cambridge, Mass.,
c1907 by George Reginald Margetson.
(22) pages.
ABSpl   NYPLS

MARGETSON, GEORGE REGINALD.
The Fledgling Bard and the Poetry Society, by George
Reginald Margetson. Boston, Richard G. Badger. (c1916).
111 pages.
ABSpl   NYPLS

MARGETSON, GEORGE REGINALD.
Songs of Life, by George Reginald Margetson.   Boston,
Sherman, French and Company, 1910.
57 pages.
ABSpl   NYPLS   DLC

MARSHALL, FLORENCE E.
Are You Awake? By Florence E. Marshall. Lansing, Michigan, Shaw Publishing Company (c1936).
96 pages.
ABSpl

MASK, W. E.
Whispers from Heaven and Melodies of the Heart. By Rev.
W. E. Mask, 140 D Street, S. E., Washington, D. C. (No im-
print).
27 pages.
HPSpl

MEANS, ST. ELMO.
Rev. St. Elmo Means' Poems, Essays, Musings and Quotations. Edited by Rev. St. Elmo Means. (n.p. c1920).
97 pages.
ABSpl

MEANS, STERLING M.
The Black Devils and Other Poems. Pentecostal Publishing Company, Louisville, Kentucky (1919).
56 pages.
HE

MEANS, STERLING M.
The Deserted Cabin and Other Poems. Atlanta, Ga., A. B.
Caldwell Co., 1915.
96 pages.
ABSpl   DLC   NYPLS

MENARD, JOHN WILLIS.
Lays in Summer Lands. Poems, by J. Willis Menard, with
the press notices of his speech and his appearance in Con-

gress. Washington, D. C., Enterprise Publishing Company,
84 pages. Portrait.
ABSpl HE HPSpl DLC NYPLS

MERRITT, ALICE HAYDEN.
Dream Themes and Other Poems, by Alice Hayden Merritt. Philadelphia, Dorrance and Co., 1940.
57 pages.
ABSpl

MERRITT, ALICE HAYDEN.
Psalms and Proverbs. A Poetical Version, by Alice Hayden Merritt. Philadelphia, Dorrance and Company, (1941).
64 pages.
ABSpl DLC

MERRIWEATHER, CLAYBRON W.
Goober Peas, by Claybron W. Merriweather. Boston, The
Christopher Publishing House (c1932).
174 pages.
ABSpl DHU DLC HE HPSpl NYPLS

MERRIWEATHER, CLAYBRON W.
The Pleasures of Life, Lyrics of the Lowly, Essays, and
Other Poems, by Claybron W. Merriweather. Hopkins-
ville, Ky., The New Era Printing Company, 1931.
156 pages.
DLC HE NYPLS

MIDDLETON, HENRY DAVIS.
Dreams of an Idle Hour, by Henry Davis Middleton. (Chi-
cago, Advocate Publishing Co., c1908).
71 pages.
"Bits of Fiction" pages 50-71.
ABSpl

MILLER, KELLY.
A Moral Axiom. (N.p., n.d.) Folio.
DHU

MILLER, LINDLEY.
Song of the First of Arkansas. No imprint. Published by
the Supervisory Committee for Recruiting Colored Regi-
ments. Broadside. 6x9½ in.
HPSpl

MILLS, THELMA.
A Book of Common Sense Poems. Composed by Thelma
Mills.s Book No. 1 (no imprint).
10 pages.
HPSpl

MILLS, THELMA.
A Book of Six Common Sense Poems. (New York, Gaillard Press, Inc. 262 W. 135th Street, n.d.)
10 pages.
HPSpl

MILLS, THELMA.
Six Poems. Book Three. (New York, Printed by Type-Art Press, 256 W. 116th Street) 1942.
8 pages.
HPSpl

MOODY, CHRISTINA.
The Story of the Easy St. Louis Riot, by Christina Moody. (No imprint) c1917.
5 unnumbered pages. Portrait.
HPSpl

MOODY, CHRISTINA.
A Tiny Spark, by Christina Moody. Washington, D. C., Murray Brothers Press, 1910.
43 pages. Portrait.
DLC HPSpl

MOORER, LIZELIA AUGUSTA JENKINS.
Prejudice Unveiled and Other Poems, by Lizelia Augusta Jenkins Moorer. Boston, Roxburgh Publishing Co., 1907.
170 pages. Portrait.
ABSpl DLC DHU

MORRIS, JOHN DAVID.
Nature's Meditations; A Book of Verses, by John David Morris. (Toledo, Ohio, The Author, c1922).
32 pages.
DHU DLC

MURPHY, BEATRICE M., ED.
Negro Voices. An Anthology of Contemporary Verse, edited by Beatrice Murphy. New York, Henry Harrison, 1938.
173 (3 unnumbered leaves) pages.
ABSpl DHU NYPLS HPSpl

NAILOR, ALEXANDER J.
Divinely Inspired Message Poems. (n.p.) Published by the Author, 1922.
59 pages. Portrait.
NYPLS

NEGRO'S PRAYER, THE. (Penned by a black man, a slave in the lower part of Virginia and written in 1790). In Equiano, Olaudah. Life and Adventures of Olaudah Equiano; or, Gustavus Vassa, the African, from an account written by

himself, abridged from A. Mott. To which are added some remarks on the slave trade. .... New York, Published by Samuel Wood and Sons. 1829.
36 pages.
NYPLS   HE

NEWSOME, EFFIE LEE.
Gladiola Garden; Poems of Outdoors and Indoors for Second Grade Readers, by Effie Lee Newsome. Illustrations by Lois Lailou Jones. Washington, D. C., The Associated Press, 1940.
167 pages.
ABSpl   DHU   NYPLS

PAISLEY, JOHN WALTER.
The Voice of Mizraim, by John Walter Paisley. New York and Washington, The Neale Publishing Co., 1907.
122 pages.
ABSpl

PATTERSON, HARRY WILSON.
Gems of the Soul; A book of Verse and Poetic Prose, by Harry Wilson Patterson, with illustrations by the Author. Washington, D. C., Murray Brothers Printers, 1935.
40 pages.   Portrait.
DHU

PAYNE, DANIEL ALEXANDER.
Pleasures and Other Miscellaneous Poems, by Daniel Alexander Payne. Baltimore, Md., Printed by Sherwood and Company, 1850.
43 pages.
ABSpl   DHU

PEKTOR, IRENE MARI.
Golden Banners, by Irene Mari Pektor. Boston, The Christopher Publishing House, (c1941).
211 pages.
DHU   DLC

PEKTOR, IRENE MARI.
War or Peace? Poems by Irene Mari Pektor. (Oceano, California, Harbison and Harbison, c1939).
60 pages.
DLC

(PETERS, ETHEL PAULINE AND ADA TRESS.)
War Poems, by Peters Sisters (n.d.n.p.)
83 pages.
ABSpl

PLATO, ANN.
Essays; including Biographies and Miscellaneous Pieces, in Prose and Poetry, by Ann Plato, introduction by James W. C. Pennington. Hartford, printed for the Author, 1841. 122 pages. Poetry on pages 93-122.
ABSpl DLC HE HPSpl NYPLS

POPEL, ESTHER, See SHAW, ESTHER POPEL.

PORTER, G. W.
Race Poems, by G. W. Porter. Containing Poems on Race Progress, Easter Festivals, Christmas Times, and Other Miscellaneous Writings, Intended to Inspire Hope in the Negro People. Clarksville, Tenn., Published by the Author. (N.d.)
48 pages. Portrait.
DHU

PORTER, G. W.
Streamlets of Poetry, by G. W. Porter. Philadelphia, Printed by the A.M.E. Book Concern, 1912.
87 pages. Portrait.
ABSpl HE NYPLS

POSEY, EDWIN.
The Voice of the Negro in South Carolina; Poems, by Edwin Posey, Columbia, S. C., The Crescent Printing Co. (c1917).
54 pages.
DLC

RAGLAND, JAMES FARLEY.
The Home Town Sketch Book. "It Happened Here." A Souvenir of Brunswick Incidents; of dale and hill in Laurenceville, and St. Paul School events, by J. Farley Ragland. Laurenceville, Va., The Brunswick Times-Gazette Press, 1940.
76 pages.
ABSpl DHU HE NYPLS SABpl

RAGLAND, JAMES FARLEY.
Lyrics and Laughter, a Volume of Contemporary (!) Verse, by J. Farley Ragland. (Lawrenceville, Va.), The Brunswick Times-Gazette Press (c1939).
90 pages. Portrait.
ABSpl DLC SABpl NYPLS

RATCLIFFE, THEODORE P.
Black Forever More. Okolona, Mississippi, Published by Okolona Industrial School, 1939.
36 pages. Portrait.
ABSpl

RAY, HENRIETTA CORDELIA.
Lincoln Written for the Occasion of the Unveiling of the Freedman's Monument in Memory of Abraham Lincoln, April 14, 1876, by H. Cordelia Ray. New York, Press of J. J. Little and Company, 1893.
11 pages.
DHU DLC

RAY, HENRIETTE CORDELIA.
Poems, by H. Cordelia Ray. New York, The Grafton Press, 1910.
169 pages.
ABSpl DHU DLC HE HPSpl NYPLS

RAY, HENRIETTE CORDELIA.
Sonnets, by Henrietta Cordelia Ray. New York, Press of J. J. Little and Company, 1893.
29 pages.
DHU DLC

REYNOLDS, EVELYN CRAWFORD.
No Alabaster Box and Other Poems. Philadelphia, Alpress, 1936.
37 pages.
ABSpl

RHODES, JACOB.
The Nation's Loss. A Poem on the Life and Death of the Hon. Abraham Lincoln, late President of the United States, who Departed this Life in Washington, D. C., April 15, 1865, by Jacob Rhodes. Newark, N. J., J. Starbuck, printer, 1866.
18 pages. Prose on pages 9-18.
DLC

RICHARDS, ELIZABETH DAVIS.
The Peddler of Dreams and Other Poems, by Elizabeth Davis Richards. New York, William Albert Broder, c1928.
96 pages.
AU

RICHARDSON, WILLIS YOUNG.
Echoes from the Negro Soul, by Willis Young Richardson. (No imprint, 1926).
99 pages. Portrait.
DHU ABSpl

RIDOUT, DANIEL LYMAN.
Verses from a Humble Cottage, by Daniel Lyman Ridout. (Hampton, Va., Hampton Institute Press, 1924).
28 pages.
ABSpl DLC NYPLS

RILEY, JAMES W.
In Memory of Departed Friends by James W. Riley. Washington, D. C., Murray Bros. Press, 1914.
48(2) pages.
HPSpl

ROGERS, ELYMAS PAYSON.
A Poem of the Fugitive Slave Law, by Rev. E. P. Rogers. Newark, N. J., A. Stephen Holbrook, Printer, 1855.
11 pages.
DHU

ROGERS, ELYMAS PAYSON.
The Repeal of the Missouri Compromise Considered, by Rev. E. P. Rogers. Newark, N. J., A Stephen Holbrook, Printer, 1856.
24 pages.
DHU   DLC

ROMEO, FRANK J.
To David W. Parker, Most Worshipful Grand Master and the Prince Hall Grand Lodge of the State of New York. This Masonic Collection of Odes is by the M. W. Grand Master's Permission Fraternally Dedicated. Compiled from the Masonic Concordia, etc., by Frank J. Romeo: Org. Carthaginian Lodge, No. 47.
(5) pages.
ABSpl

ROWE, GEORGE CLINTON.
A Noble Life. Memorial Souvenir of Rev. Jos. C. Price, by Geo. C. Rowe. Charleston, S. C., 1894.
7 pages.
NYPLS

ROWE, GEORGE C(LINTON).
Our Heroes. Patriotic Poems on Men, Women and Satings of the Negro Race, by George C. Rowe. Charleston, S. C., Walker Evans & Cogswell Co., Printers, 1890.
68 pages.
DHU

ROWE, GEORGE CLINTON.
Thoughts in Verse. A Volume of Poems, by George Clinton Rowe. Charleston, S. C., Kahrs Stolze & Welch Printers, 1887.
113 pages. Portrait.
ABSpl   DLC   HPSpl   NYPLS

ROWLAND, IDA.
Lisping Leaves, by Ida Rowland. Philadelphia, Dorance and Company (1939).
55 pages.
ABSpl   DHU

67

SAMUEL, AARON.
Helping Hand. New York, (1905).
77(3) pages. Portrait.
NYPLS

SAVAGE, EUDORA V.
Vibrations of My Heart. New York, The Exposition Press,
1944.
96 pages.
DHU

SCOTT, EMORY ELROGE.
Lyrics of the Southland, by E. E. Scott. (Chicago, c. by W.
F. Scott, 1913).
93 pages.
ABSpl

SCOTT, RALEIGH ALONZO.
Scott's Poetic Gems, by Alonzo R. Scott; A Choice Collec-
tion of His Best Poems including his Great Master Piece
and Prize Winners—Echoes of Emancipation, The World
Safe for Democracy, Count the Negro in, Uncle Sam's
Dream, How Aunt Dinah "Got By," etc. etc. Opelika, Ala.,
J. B. Ware, agent, c1918.
44 pages. Portrait.
DLC

SEVEN POETS in Search of an Answer. .... A Poetic Sym-
posium edited by Thomas Yoseloff. With an Introduction
note by Shaemas A. Sheel. New York, Bernard Ackerman
(c1944).
118 pages. Ten poems of Langston Hughes included.
ABSpl

SEWARD, WALTER EDDIE.
Negroes call to the colors and Soldiers Camp-Life Poems
(by) Private Walter E. Seward. .... Athens, Ga., Knox Institute Press, 1919.
112 pages. Portrait.
DLC

SHACKELFORD, OTIS M.
Seeking the Best. Dedicated to the Negro Youth by Otis
M. S. Shackleford. Kansas City, Mo., Franklin Hudson
Publishing Co., 1909.
177 pages. Portrait. Verse and prose.
NYPLS   DLC
Also: Kansas City, Mo., 1913.
HE

SHACKELFORD, THEODORE HENRY.
Mammy's Cracklin' Bread and other Poems, by Theodore

Henry Shackelford. Philadelphia, Press of I. W. Klopp Co., 1916.
58 pages. Portrait.
ABSpl HPSpl NYPLS

SHACKELFORD, THEODORE HENRY.
My Country and Other Poems, by Theodore Henry Shackelford. Illustrated by the Author. (Philadelphia, Press of I. W. Klopp Co., c1916-18).
216 pages. Portrait.
ABSpl DHU HE HPSpl NYPLS

SHACKELFORD, WILLIAM H.
Pearls in Prose and Poetry, by William H. Shackelford. Nashville, Tenn., National Baptist Publishing Board, 1907.
82 pages. Portrait.
HPSpl NYPLS

Schomburg lists: Poems. Nashville, Tenn., 1915. This has not been located.

SHADWELL, BERTRAND.
America and Other Poems. Chicago, R. R. Donnelley and Sons Co., 1899.
82 pages.
The compiler could not verify this author as a Negro. "Mulatto" had been written in on the title page of the copy in the Henry P. Slaughter private collection.
DLC HPSpl

(SHAW, ESTHER POPEL).
A Forest Pool, by Esther Popel. Washington, D. C. Privately Printed. (Modernistic Press), 1934.
42 pages.
ABSpl DLC

(SHAW, ESTHER POPEL).
Thoughtless Thinks by a Thinkless Thoughter. Rhymes by Esther A. B. Popel.
16 pages.
ABSpl

SHOEMAN, CHARLES HENRY.
A Dream and Other Poems, by Charles Henry Shoeman. 2d ed. Ann Arbor, Published by George Wahr, 1899.
202 pages. Portrait.
ABSpl NYPLS

SIDNEY, R. Y.
Anthems Composed for the National Jubilee of the Abolition of the Slave Trade, January 1, 1809.
In Sidney, Joseph. An Oration, Commemorative of the

Abolition of the Slave Trade in the United States. _____ New York, Printed for the Author, J. Seymour, printer. 1809. (19)-20 pages.
ABSpl   DLC   NYHS

SIMMONS, VIRGINIA.
Whitecaps, (by) Virginia Simmons. (Yellow Springs, Ohio, Printed by the Antioch, Press, 1942).
79 pages.
ABSpl   NYPLS

SIMPSON, JOSHUA McCARTER.
The Emancipation Car, Being an Original Composition of Anti-Slavery Ballads, Composed Exclusively for the Under Ground Railroad, by J. McC. Simpson.   Zanesville, O., Printed by Sullivan and Brown, 1874.
152(4) pages.
DHU

SING, LAUGH, WEEP. A Book of Poems by the Scribes. With Illustrations by Theopolus Williams.   St. Louis, Press Publishing Co., 1944.
126 pages.
DHU

SLUBY, M. F.
Satire. Lines Suggested on Reading the Confession of Dr. B. T. Tanner, editor of the "Christian Recorder." By M. F. Sluby, December 8th, 1881, and May 11th, 1883. Philadelphia, Pa.
8 pages.
ABSpl

SMITH, J. PAULINE.
"Exceeding Riches" and Other Verse, by J. Pauline Smith. Detroit, Michigan, 1922.
89 pages.
DLC

SMITH, J. PAULINE, COMPILER.
Olive Prints, Selections from Robert Browning's Poems for Every Day in the Year, compiled by J. Pauline Smith, 1903. Detroit Press of William Graham Printing Co. (c1903).
95 pages.
HPSpl

SMITH, S. P.
Our Alma Mater and Other Poems, by S. P. Smith of Fayetteville, North Carolina. (Washington, D. C., c1904, by Rev. A. C. Garner).
(25) pages. Portrait.
DHU

STANFORD, THEODORE ANTHONY.
Dark Harvest, by Theodore Anthony Stanford, with an introduction by Joseph V. Baker. Philadelphia (Published by Bureau on Negro Affairs, 1519 Lombard Street, 1936.)
32 pages.
ABSpl   AU   DHU   HPSpl   NYPLS

TALLEY, THOMAS WASHINGTON.
Negro Folk Rhymes, Wise and Otherwise. With a Study by Thomas W. Talley. New York, The MacMillan Company, 1922.
347 pages.
ABSpl   DHU   HE   HPSpl

TANNER, BENJAMIN TUCKER.
Stray Thoughts. (No imprint).
20 pages.
HPSpl

TANNER, B(ENJAMIN) T(UCKER).
To the Memory of Professor O. V. Catto. Respectfully Inscribed to His Fellows of the Institute for Colored Youth, and to the Pupils of the Same, with Consideration. (No imprint). Folio.
HPSpl   NYPLS

TEMPLE, GEORGE HANNIBAL.
The Epic of Columbus' Bell and Other Poems, by George Hannibal Temple. Reading, Pa., Press of the Reading Eagle, 1900.
80 pages. Portrait.
DLC   HPSpl   NYPLS

THOMAS, CHARLES CYRUS.
A Black Lark Caroling, by Charles Cyrus Thomas. Dallas, Texas, The Kaleidograph Press, (1936).
73 pages.
ABSpl   DHU   NYPLS

THOMAS, CHARLES CYRUS.
Sweet Land of Liberty, a Book of Poems, by Charles Cyrus Thomas. Ravenna, Ohio, The Author, 402 Jefferson Street, (1937).
6 pages.
ABSpl   DHU   NYPLS

THOMAS, JAMES HENRY.
Sentimental and Comical Poems, by James H. Thomas. Nashville, Tenn. National Baptist Publishing Board, 1913.
171 pages. Portrait.
DLC   HPSpl   NYPLS

THOMPSON, AARON BELFORD.
Echoes of Spring, by Aaron Belford Thompson. Rossmoyne,
Ohio, Printed and for sale by the Author, 1901.
76 pages. Portrait.
ABSpl DLC

THOMPSON, AARON BELFORD.
Harvest of Thoughts, by Aaron Belford Thompson ....
with an introduction by James Whitcomb Riley. Illustrated by G. T. Haywood. Indianapolis, Ind., The Author,
c1907.
110 pages. Portrait.
ABSpl DLC

THOMPSON, AARON BELFORD.
Morning Songs, by Aaron Belford Thompson. Rossmoyne,
Ohio, Privately Printed, 1899.
82 pages. Portrait.
ABSpl DLC

THOMPSON, CLARA ANN.
A Garland of Poems, by Clara Ann Thompson. Boston.
The Christopher Publishing House (c1926).
96 pages. Portrait.
ABSpl DHU DLC HPSpl NYPLS

THOMPSON, CLARA ANN.
Songs from the Wayside, by Clara Ann Thompson. Rossmoyne, O., The Author, 1908.
96 pages. Portrait.
ABSpl DLC NYPLS

THOMPSON, JOSEPH.
"Songs of Caroline," by Joseph Thompson. Chicago, Ill.,
Joseph Thompson, 4732 Indiana Ave. (1936).
30 pages. Portrait.
ABSpl

THOMPSON, PRISCILLA JANE.
Ethiope Lays, by Priscilla Jane Thompson. Rosswoyne,
Ohio, The Author, 1900.
95 pages. Portrait.
ABSpl DLC NYPLS

THOMPSON, PRISCILLA JANE.
Gleanings of Quiet Hours, by Priscilla Jane Thompson.
Rossmoyne, O., The Author, c1907.
100 pages. Portrait.
ABSpl DLC NYPLS

THORNE, J. ALBERT.
The Dew of Hermon or Dwelling Together in Unity, An

Ode to Two Devoted Sisters. Toronto, Canada, The Methodist Book and Publishing House, 1920.
15 pages.
HPSpl

THORNTON, GEORGE BENNETT.
Best Poems of George B. Thornton (c1937).
27 pages. Portrait.
ABSpl

TINDLEY, J. C., ED.
Poems and Writings of the Late Rev. Chas. Albert Tinidley.
Philadelphia, Pa., Published by Mrs. J. C. Tindley (n.d.).
38 pages. Portrait.
HPSpl

TODD, WALTER E.
Fireside Musings, by Walter E. Todd. Washington, D. C., Published by Murray Brothers, 1908.
52(1) pages. Portrait.
ABSpl   DHU

TODD, WALTER E.
Fireside Musings, by Walter E. Todd, 2d ed. Washington, D. C., The Murray Brothers Press, 1909.
52(1) pages. Portrait.
ABSpl   HPSpl   NYPLS

TODD, WALTER E.
Gathered Treasures, by Walter E. Todd, 1st ed. Washington, D. C., Murray Brothers Printing Company, 1912.
39(1) pages. Portrait.
DHU   HE   HPSpl

TODD, WALTER E.
Gathered Treasures. 4th ed. Washington, D. C., Murray Brothers Printing Company, 1915.
40 pages. Portrait.
ABSpl

TODD, WALTER E.
A Little Sunshine, by Walter E. Todd. Washington, D. C., Murray Brothers Printing Company (c1917).
63 pages. Portrait.
ABSpl DHU HPSpl   NYPLS
Also: Washington, 1923.
HE

TODD, WALTER E.
Parson Johnson's Lecture, by Walter E. Todd. Washington, D. C., Murray Brothers, Printers, 1906.
45 pages. Portrait.
ABSpl

TODD, WALTER E.
Young Men's Christian Association. A Poem, by Walter
E. Todd. Washington, D. C., Oscar D. Morris, Printer, 1905.
4 unnumbered leaves.
DHU

TOLSON, MELVIN B.
Rendezvous With America, by Melvin B. Tolson. New
York, Dodd, Mead and Company, 1944.
121 pages.
ABSpl   HE

TOMLIN, J. HENRI.
Varied Verses. A Book of Poems by J. Henri Tomlin. (c by
the author, 1937).
92 pages.
ABSpl

TOOMEY, RICHARD E. S.
Thoughts for True Americans, a Book of Poems, dedicat-
ed to the Lovers of American Ideals, by Richard E. Toomey.
Washington, D. C., The Neale Publishing Company, 1901.
80 pages.
DHU HPSpl NYPLS

TURNER, LUCY MAE.
'Bout Cullud Folkses, Poems by Lucy Mae Turner. New
York, Henry Harrison (c1938).
64 pages.
ABSpl DHU   HE NYPLS

TYLER, EPHRAIM DAVID.
Tyler's Poems. Poems of Every Day Life, by Ephraim
David Tyler. (Shreveport, La., The Author, n.d.).
44 pages.
SABpl

UNDERHILL, IRWIN W.
The Brown Madonna and Other Poems, by Irwin W. Underhill, Philadelphia, Pa. (c1929).
95 pages.
ABSpl

UNDERHILL, IRWIN W.
Daddy's Love and Other Poems, by Irvin W. Underhill.
Philadelphia, Pa. (A.M.E. Book Concern Printers. n.d.)
87 pages.
ABSpl DHU   HPSpl NYPLS

USSERY, AMOS A.
The Negro Says, by Amos A. Ussery. (Little Rock, Arkansas, The Author, n.d.)
(10) pages. Portrait.
SABpl

74

(VANCE, HART).
Cui Bono? (n.p. 1919).
12 pages.
ABSpl

VANDYNE, WILLIAM JOHNSON.
Revels of Fancy, by William Johnson Vandyne. ...... Boston, A. F. Grant, Publisher, 1891.
55 pages.
ABSpl

WALDEN. ISLAY.
Walden's Miscellaneous Poems, Which the Author Desires to Dedicate to the Cause of Education and Humanity. Washington, Reed and Woodward, printers, 1872.
50 pages.
DLC

(WALDEN, ISLAY).
Walden's Miscellaneous Poems which the Author Desires to Dedicate to the Cause of Education and Humanity. 2nd ed. Washington, Published by the Author, 1873.
96 pages.
DHU   ABSpl   DLC   NYPLS

WALDEN, ISLAY.
Walden's Sacred Poems, with a Sketch of His Life. .... New Brunswick, N. J., Terhune and Van Anglen's press, 1877.
23 pages.
DLC   NYHS

WALKER, JAMES R(OBERT).
Poetical Diets, by James R. Walker. (No imprint).
146 pages. Portrait.
DHU   NYPLS

WALKER, MARGARET.
For My People, by Margaret Walker. New Haven, Yale University Press. 1942.
58 pages.
ABSpl   DHU   DLC   HPSpl   NYPLS

WALKER, WILLIAM.
Mother's Day Special Poem Book, by William Walker. Chicago, Ill., Published by William Walker, 520 E. 40th Street, 1941.
12 pages.
DHU   HE

WALKER, WILLIAM.
Poem Book Number Ten of Every Day Life Poetry. Chicago, c1943. n.p.
20 pages. Portrait.
HE HPSpl

WALKER, WILLIAM.
Poem Book of Inspirational Thoughts. Chicago, Ill., Published by William Walker, 520 E. 40th St., 1940.
16 pages.
DHU HE

WALKER, WILLIAM.
Poetical Biography of William Walker, Poet, Author and Dramatic Reader. Chicago, Ill., Published by Wm. Walker, 520 E. 40th St. (n.d.).
2 pages. Portrait.
DHU HE

WALKER, WILLIAM.
Walker's Book of Original Poems. Chicago, Ill., Published by Jones and Co., 19 W. 39th St., 1939.
25 pages.
DHU HE

WALKER, WILLIAM.
Walker's Every Day Life Poetry Book. Chicago, Ill., Published by S. L. White Co., 3814 S. State St., 1936.
69 pages.
DHU HE

WALKER, WILLIAM.
Walker's Humorous Poem Book. Chicago, Ill., Published by William Walker, 520 E. 40th St., 1940.
16 pages.
DHU HE

WALKER, WILLIAM.
Walker's No. 1 All Occasion Poem Book. New York, The Exposition Press, 1940.
32 pages.
DHU HE

WALKER, WILLIAM.
Walker's No. 2 All Occasion Poem Book; Every Day Life Poetry, by William Walker. Chicago, William Walker, Publisher, c1944.
206 pages. Portrait.
HE HPSpl

WALKER, WILLIAM.
Walker's No. 8 Poem Book. Chicago, Ill., Published by
William Walker, 520 E. 40th St., 1942.
16 pages.
DHU   HE

WALKER, WILLIAM.
Walker's No. 9 Poem Book. Chicago, Ill., Published by
William Walker, 520 E. 40th St., 1943.
20 pages.
DHU   HE

WALLER, EFFIE.
Rhymes from the Cumberland, by Effie Waller. New York,
Broadway Publishing Co., (c1909).
53 pages. Portrait.
DLC   NYPLS

WALLER, EFFIE.
Songs of the Months, by Effie Waller. New York, Published by Broadway Pub. Co., 1904.
175 pages.
NYPLS

WARD, ELLA J. MAYO.
Bougainvilles and Desert Sand, by Ella J. Mayo Ward.
Charlottesville, Va., The Michie Company, Printers, 1942.
72 pages. Portrait.
DLC

WARD, ELLA J. MAYO.
Purple Wings; A Book of Verse, by Ella J. Mayo Ward.
Charlottesville, Va.,' The Michie Company, Printers, 1941.
87 pages. Portrait.
DLC   NYPLS

WARRICK, C. HORATIO.
The True Criteria and Other Poems, by C. Horatio Warrick. Kansas City, Missouri, The Sojourner Press, 1924.
120 pages. Portrait.
ABSpl

WATKINS, LUCIAN B(OTTOW).
Voices of Solitude, Poems Written and Composed by
Lucian B. Watkins. Chicago, M. A. Donohue and Co.,
(c1903).
128 pages. Portrait.
DLC   NYPLS

WESTFIELD, CHESTER J.
The Experiences of Company "L," 368th Infantry, a Unit
of the Black Buffalo Division, Told in Verse Typical of a

Soldier's Life in France _____ by Sgt. Chester J. Westfield.
Nashville, Hemphill Press, (1919).
8 pages.
DLC

WHEATLEY, PHILLIS.
An elegiac poem, on the death of that celebrated divine,
and eminent servant of Jesus Christ, the late Reverend,
and pious George Whitefield, Chaplain to the right Honourable the Countess of Huntingdon, etc, etc. Who made
his exit from this transitory state, to dwell in the celestial
realms of bliss, on Lord's-day, 30th of September 1770,
when he was seiz'd with a fit of asthma, at Newbury-Port,
near Boston in New Engnland. In which is a condolatory
address to his noble benefactress the worthy, and pious
Lady Huntingdon; and the orphan-children in Georgia;
who with many thousands, are left, by the death of this
great man, to lament the loss of a father, and benefactor.
By Phillis, a servant girl 17 years of age, belonging to Mr.
J. Wheatley, of Boston; and has been but 9 years in this
country from Africa. Bcston: sold by Ezekial Russell, in
Queen-Street, and John Boyles, in Marlboro'-Street, (1770).
Broadside.
LCP

WHEATLEY, PHILLIS.
An elegiac poem, on the death of that celebrated divine,
and eminent servant of Jesus Christ, the late Reverend,
and pious George Whitefield, Chaplain to the right Honourable the Countess of Huntington, etc., etc. Who made
his exit from this transitory state, to dwell in the celestial
realm of bliss, on Lord's-day, 30th of September, 1770, when
he was seized with a fit of asthma, at Newbury-Port, near
Boston, in New England. In which is a condolatory address to his truly noble benefactress the worthy and pious
Lady Huntingdon, and the orphan-children in Georgia;
who, with many thousands are sic. left, by the death of
this great man, to lament the loss of a father, friend and
benefactor. By Phillis, a servant girl of 17 years of age,
belonging to Mr. J. Wheatley, of Boston; and has been but
9 years in this country from Africa. (1770).
Broadside. 25x38cm.
PHS

WHEATLEY, PHILLIS.
An elegiac poem, on the death of that celebrated divine,
and eminent servant of Jesus Christ, the Reverend and
learned George Whitefield, chaplain to the Right Honourable the Countess of Huntingdon, etc., etc., who made his
exit from this transitory state, to dwell in the celestial
realms of bliss, on Lord's day, 30th of September, 1770,

when he was seiz'd with a fit of the ashtma, at Newbury-Port, near Boston, New England. In which is a condolatory address to his truly noble benefactress the worthy and pious Lady Huntingdon; and the orphan children in Georgia, who, with many thousands are left, by the death of this great man, to lament the loss of a father, friend and benefactor. By Phillis, a servant girl, of 17 years of age, belonging to Mr. J. Wheatley, of Boston: She has been but 9 years in this country from Africa. Boston: Printed and sold by Ezekial Russell, in Queen-Street, and John Boyles, in Marlboro's Street. (1770).
8 pages.
HCL DLC LCRB NYHS NYPL
added t.-p., illus.

WHEATLEY, PHILLIS.
An elegiac poem on the death of George Whitefield. (In Pemberton, Ebenezer). Heaven the Residence of Saints. A sermon occasioned by the sudden and much lamented death of the Rev. George Whitefield, A.M., Chaplain to the right honourable the Countess of Huntington. Delivered at the Thursday lecture in Boston, in America. October 11, 1770, by Ebenezer Pemberton, D.D., Pastor of a church in Boston, to which is added, an elegiac pcem on his death, by Phillis, a Negro girl, of seventeen years of age, belonging to Mr. John Wheatley of Boston. Boston, Printed: London reprinted for E. and C. Dilly in the Poultry; and sold at the chapel in Tottenham-Court Road, and at the Tabernacle near Moorfields. 1771.
(29)-31 pages.
AAS ABSpl BA BU DHU JCB HE MHS NYPL
NYPLS NYHS PU HCL YU

WHEATLEY, PHILLIS.
An elegy, sacred to the memory of that great Divine, the Reverend and learned Dr. Samuel Cooper, who departed this life December 29, 1783, Aetatis 59. By Phillis Peters. Boston: Printed and sold by E. Russell in Essex-Street, near Liberty-Pole, 1784.
(6) pages.
AAS ABSpl BA MHS NYHS

WHEATLEY, PHILLIS.
Liberty and Peace, a poem, by Phillis Peters, 1753-1784. Printed by Warden and Russell, at their office in Marlborough-Street, 1784.
4 pages, 22cm. E18727.
AAS HCE NYHS

WHEATLEY, PHILLIS.
Life and Works of Phillis Wheatley, Containing her Complete Poetical Works, Numerous Letters, and a Complete

Biography of this Famous Poet of a Century and a Half Ago, by G. Herbert Renfro. Also a Sketch of the Life of Mr. Renfro, by Leila Amos Pendleton. Washington, D. C., (Published by Robert L. Pendleton) 1916.
112 pages. Portrait.
DHU NYPLS HPSpl ABSpl

WHEATLEY, PHILLIS.
Memoir and Poems, of Phillis, a Native African and Slave. Dedicated to the Friends of the Africans. (Four lines of quotation). Boston: Published by George Light, Lyceum Depository, 3 Cornhill, 1834.
4 p.l. (46)-103p. Portrait.
AAS ABSpl BA BPL DHU DLC MHS NYHS

WHEATLEY, PHILLIS.
Memoir and poems of Phillis Wheatley, a native African and slave. Dedicated to the friends of Africans. (Four lines of quotations). Second edition. Boston: Light and Horton, 1 and 3 Cornhill, Samuel Harris, Printer, 1835.
viii, (1) 10-114 pages. Portrait.
AAS HE HPS MHS NYPLS NYHS YU

WHEATLEY, PHILLIS.
Phillis Wheatley (Phillis Peters) Poems and Letters, First collected edition. Edited by Chas. Fred. Heartman. With an appreciation by Arthur Schomburg. New York, Chas. Fred. Heartman, Portrait.
An edition of forty copies printed on Fabriano Handmade paper.
HE NYPLS (No. 19)

WHEATLEY, PHILLIS.
Phillis Wheatley (Phillis Peters) Poems and Letters. First collected edition. Edited by Chas. Fred. Heartman. With an appreciation by Arthur Schomburg. New York, Chas. Fred. Heartman, (n.d.) Portrait.
An edition of four hundred copies, of which nine were printed on Japan vellum paper.
ABSpl (No. 4) DHU (No. 7) HE NYPLS (No. 5)

WHEATLEY, PHILLIS.
Phillis Wheatley (Phillis Peters). A Critical Attempt and a Bibliography of Her Writings, by Charles Fred. Heartman. New York (Chas. Fred. Heartman) 1915.
An edition of eight copies printed on Japan vellum.
HE (No. 1) NYPLS (No. 8)

WHEATLEY, PHILLIS.
Phillis Wheatley (Phiillis Peters). A Critical Attempt and a Bibliography of her Writings, by Charles Fred. Heartman.

New York, (Chas. Fred. Heartman) 1915.
An edtion of 91 copies.
HE   NYPLS (No. 73)

WHEATLEY, PHILLIS.
Phillis' poem on the death of Mr. Whitefield. (Boston, 1770).
Broadside. 12x34cm.
AAS
Contains also: "Bedlam Garland. Together with the Spin-
ning Wheel."

WHEATLEY, PHILLIS.
Poems on various subjects, religious and moral. By Phillis Wheatley, Negro servant to Mr. John Wheatley, of Boston, in New England. London: Printed for A. Bell, Bookseller, Aldgate; and sold by Messrs. Cox and Berry, King
Street, Boston. MDCCLXXIII.
124(4) pages.
AAS ASPpl BPL HCL DLC DHU HE NYHS
NYPLS   YU

WHEATLEY, PHILLIS.
Poems on various subjects, religious and moral, by Phillis
Wheatley, Negro servant to Mr. John Wheatley. of Boston,
in New England. London: Printed. Philadelphia: Reprinted, and sold by Joseph Crukshank, in Market Street, between Second and Third Streets. 1786.
vi, (2) (9)-66, (2) pages.
LC PHS (Joseph Lloyd's book-1789) NYHS ABSpl
First American edition.

WHEATLEY, PHILLIS.
Poems on various subjects, religious and moral, by Phillis
Wheatley, Negro servant to Mr. John Wheatley, of Boston,
in New England. Philadelphia: Printed by Joseph James,
in Chestnut Street. MDCCLXXXVII.
55, (2) pages.
AAS DLC ABSpl

WHEATLEY, PHILLIS.
Poems on various subjects, religious and moral, by Phillis
Wheatley, Negro servant to Mr. John Wheatley, of Boston,
in New England. London: Printed, Philadelphia: Reprinted,
and sold by Joseph Crukshank, in Market street, between
Second and Third streets. MDCCLXXXIx.
vi, (2) (9)-86, (2) pages.
AAS DLC

WHEATLEY, PHILLIS.
Poems on various subjects, religious and moral, by Phillis
Wheatley, Negro servant to Mr. John Wheatley, of Boston,
in New England. Albany: Reprinted from the London edi-

tion, by Barber and Southwick, for Thomas Spencer, Bookseller, Market-Street, 1793.
viii, 88, 3 pages.
AAS ABSpl BU DLC NYPL

WHEATLEY, PHILLIS.
Poems on various subjects, moral and entertaining; by Phillis Wheatley, Negro servant to Mr. John Wheatley, of Boston, in New-England.
(In Lavallee, Joseph, marquis de Bois-Robert. The Negro equalled by few Europeans. Translated from the French. To which are added, Poems on various subjects, moral and entertaining; by Phillis Wheatley, Negro servant to Mr. John Wheatley, of Boston, in New-England. Philadelphia: Printed by and for William W. Woodward, No. 17, Chestnut Street, 1801. vol. II.)
AAS BPL DLC CFH MHS NYPL

WHEATLEY, PHILLIS.
Poems on various subjects, religious and moral, by Phillis Wheatley, Negro servant to Mr. John Wheatley, of Boston, in New-England. Dedicated to the Countess of Huntingdon. Walpole, N. H. Printed for Thomas & Thomas, by Davis Newhall, 1802.
86 pages.
AAS (autographed) BA BPL HE HCL DLC MHS NYHS NYPLS ABSP

WHEATLEY, PHILLIS.
Poems on various subjects, religious and moral, by Phillis Wheatley, Negro servant to the late Mr. John Wheatley, of Boston (Mass.) Hartford: Printed by Oliver Steele, 1804.
92(2) pages.
AAS YU

WHEATLEY, PHILLIS.
Poemss, on various subjects, religious and moral, by Phillis Wheatley, Negro servant to Mr. John Wheatley, of Boston, in New-England. London: Printed. Re-printed, in New-England. 1816.
120 pages.
AAS ABSpl BPL HE NYHS NYPLS YU

WHEATLEY, PHILLIS.
Poems on Various Subjects, Religious and Moral, by Phillis Wheatley, Negro servant to Mr. John Wheatley, of Boston, in New England. With Memoirs by W. H. Jackson, Denver, Colo., W. H. Laurence & Co., 1887.
147 pages. Portrait.
Poetry, p. 1-116. Memoir, p. 117-125. p. 126-147, Memoirs of Benjamin Banneker, Thomas Fuller and James Durham.
NYPLS

WHEATLEY, PHILLIS.
The Poems of Phillis Wheatley as they were Originally
Published in London, 1773. Re-published by R. R. and C.
C. Wright. Philadelphia, Pa., 1909.
88 pages. Portrait.
HPSpl NYPLS

WHEATLEY, PHILLIS.
The Poems of Phillis Wheatley, edited with an Introduc-
tion and Notes by Charlotte Ruth Wright. Philadelphia,
Published by the Wrights, 925 N. 48th St., 1930.
104 pages. Portrait.
NYPLS

WHEATLEY, PHILLIS.
Six Broadsides relating to Phillis Wheatley (Phillis Peters).
With Portrait and Facsimile of Her Handwriting. Twenty-
five copies Printed by Chas. Fred. Heartman, New York
City, 1915.
HE NYPLS

WHEATLEY, PHILLIS.
To Mr. and Mrs. _____ on the Death of Their Infant
Son. By Phillis Wheatly (sic). (Printed in The Boston Maga-
zine for September, 1784, p. 488).
This poem of fifty eight lines is included here because it
is not in any of the collections examined.
DHU

WHEATLEY, PHILLIS.
To Mrs. Leonard, on the death of her husband. Boston,
1771. Broadside. 23x11½cm.
MHS (Photostat) PHS
Signed Phillis Wheatley.

WHEATLEY, PHILLIS.
To the Hon'ble Thomas Hubbard, Esq., on the death of
Mrs. Thankfull Leonard. Dated, Boston, January 2, 1773,
and signed Phillis Wheatley.
Broadside. 23x30cm.
PHS MHS (Photostat)

WHEATLEY, PHILLIS.
To the Rev. Mr. Pitkin, on the death of his Lady. (1772).
Broadside. 10½x29cm. E12618.
BPL (Photostat) MHS (Photostat) NYHS
Signed Phillis Wheatley and dated Boston, June 16, 1772.

WHEELER, BENJAMIN FRANKLIN.
Cullings from Zion's Poets, by B. F. Wheeler. (Mobile, Ala.,
c1907).
384 pages. Portraits.
ABSpl DHU HPSpl NYPLS

WHITE, CHARLES FRED.
Plea of the Negro Soldier and a hundred Other Poems, by Corporal Charles Fred White, Chaplain of Wesley S. Brass Camp, No. 37, United Spanish War Veterans. Easthampton, Mass., Press of Enterprise Printing Co., (c1908).
170(2) pages. Portrait.
HE   HPSpl   NYPLS

WHITE, JAMES WILSON.
White's Poems, by James Wilson White. Washington, D. C., 1925.
94 pages.
HPSpl   DLC

WHITFIELD, JAMES M.
America and Other Poems, by J. M. Whitfield. Buffalo, Published by James S. Leavitt, 1853.
85 pages.
ABSpl   NYPLS

WHITMAN, ALBERY ALLSON.
An Idyl of the South, by Albery A. Whitman. An Epic Poem in Two Parts. New York, The Metaphysical Publishing Company, 1901.
126 pages.
ABSpl   DHU   DLC   HPSpl   NYPLS

WHITMAN, ALBERY ALLSON.
Leelah Misled. A Poem, by A. A. Whitman. Elizabethtown, Richard La Rue, printer, 1873.
39 pages.
ABSpl   NYPLS
The preface in this volume states that that Whitman also published a work entitled—Essay on the Ten Plagues, and Miscellaneous Poems "of which 1000 copies sold."

WHITMAN, ALBERY ALLSON.
Not a Man, and Yet a Man, by A. A. Whitman. Springfield, Ohio, Republic Printing Company, 1877.
254 pages. Portrait.
ABSpl   DHU   DLC   HE   HPSpl   NYPLS

WHITMAN, ALBERY ALLSON.
The Rape of Florida, by Albery A. Whitman. St. Louis, Nixon-Jones Printing Co., 1884.
95 pages. Portrait.
ABSpl   HE

WHITMAN, ALBERY ALLSON.
Twasinta's Seminoles; or, Rape of Florida, by Albery Allson Whitman. Rev. Ed. St. Louis, Nixon-Jones Printing Co., 1885.
97 pages. Portrait.
ABSpl   DLC   HE   HPSpl   NYPLS

WHITMAN, ALBERY ALLSON.
Twasinta's Seminoles; or, Rape of Florida. 3d ed., care-
fully revised. St. Louis, Nixon-Jones Printing Co., 1890.
96 pages.
ABSpl DHU NYPLS

WHITMAN, ALBERY ALLSON.
World's Fair Poem. Read in Memorial Art Palace, Chicago,
Illinois, September 22nd, 1893. Atlanta, Ga., Holsey Job
Print, 212 Auburn Avenue. 1893.
9 pages. Portrait.
Undated nine-page leaflet. Contains "The Veteran," recit-
ed by Mrs. Caddie Whitman at the World's Fair Congress
p. 8-9.
DHU NYPLS

WHITNEY, SALEM TUTT.
Mellow Musings, by Salem Tutt Whitney, with an intro-
duction by Thomas L. G. Orley. Boston, The Colored Poetic
League of the World. 1926.
126 pages. Portrait.
DHU HPSpl NYPLS

WIGGINS, BERNICE LOVE.
Tuneful Tales, by Bernice Love Wiggins. El Paso, Texas,
1925.
174 pages.
ABSpl

WILDS, MYRA VIOLA.
Thoughts of Idle Hours, by Myra Viola Wilds. Illustrations
by Lorenzo Harris, Artist. Nashville, Tenn., National Baptist Publishing Board, 1915.
81 pages. Portrait.
ABSpl HPSpl DLC NYPLS

WILKINSON, HENRY BERTRAM.
Desert Sands. A Volumn of Verse Touching Various Top-
ics. London, Arthur H. Stockwell, Ltd., n.d. (ca.1933).
ABSpl HPSpl NYPLS

WILKINSON, HENRY BERTRAM.
Idle Hours, by Henry B. Wilkinson. New York, F. H. Hit-
cock (c1927).
86 pages.
ABSpl DHU DLC HE NYPLS

WILKINSON, HENRY BERTRAM.
Shady-Rest, by Henry B. Wilkinson. New York, Frederick
H. Hitchcock (c1928).
69 pages.
ABSpl HE HPSpl NYPLS

WILKINSON, HENRY BERTRAM.
Transitory, A Poem by Henry B. Wilkinson. Dedicated to a Peaceful World. Boston, Privately Printed for the Author by the Popular Poetry Publishers (c1941).
20 pages.
ABSpl

WILLIAMS, EDWARD W.
The Views and Meditations of John Brown, by Edward W. Williams, author of Americus Moor; or, Life Among the American Freedmen. (Washington, D. C., n.d.)
16 pages.
ABSpl NYPLS

WILLIAMS, FRANK B.
Fifty Years of Freedom. (Washington, D. C., Hamilton Printing Co., 1913).
8 unnumbered leaves.
DHU

WILLIAMS, HENRY ROGER.
Are we Free? An Emancipation Day Address Written in Cadensed Verses, by H. Roger Williams. (Mobile, Ala., c1928? by the Author).
26 pages.
ABSpl

WILLIAMS, HENRY ROGER.
The Christ is a Negro, by H. Roger Williams. Mobile, Ala., c1923 by the Author.
(19) pages.
ABSpl

WILLIAMS, HENRY ROGER.
Heart Throbs; Poems of Race Inspiration, Written by H. Roger Williams, Mobile, Ala., Printed by Gulf City Printing Co., Inc., 1923.
80 pages. Portrait.
ABSpl

WILLIAMS, PETER.
Hymns Composed by Peter Williams and Sung on the Occasion of the Delivery of an Address to the New York African Society, for Mutual Relief. In Hamilton, William. An Address to the New York African Society for Mutual Relief, Delivered in the Universalist Church, January 2, 1809, by William Hamilton. New York, Printed in the Year 1809.
BA

WIT AND HUMOR, by Uncle Sambo. Edwards, Miss., The New Light Steam Print, 1911.
23 pages. Portrait.
NYPLS

WITHERSPOON, JAMES WILLIAM.

A Breath of the Muse. A Volume of Poetic Browsings, Containing Several Prose Writings, by J. William Witherspoon. Columbia, S. C., Hampton Publishing Company, 1927. 132 pages. Portrait.
ABSpl   AU   DHU

WORMLEY, BEATRICE F., AND CHARLES W. CARTER.

An Anthology of Negro Poetry by Nogroes and Others. No place, no date.
140 pages.
HE
Works Progress Administration of New Jersey.

WORMLEY, G. SMITH.

Dedicated to the Memory of Rev. W. L. Washington, Pastor, Zion Baptist Church, Washington, D. C., 1933. (No imprint).
Broadside. 9x18cm.
DHU

WORMLEY, G. SMITH.

Mother. (No imprint).
Broadside. 10x17cm.
DHU

WRIGHT, JULIUS C.

Poetic Diamonds, written for the interest of Afro-Americans and all concerned, by Julius C. Wright, a youth of twenty years, who never spent a day in college. Montgomery, Ala., W. E. Allred Printing, 1906.
64 pages. Portrait.
DLC   NYPLS

YANCEY, BESSIE WOODSON.

Echoes from the Hills, A Book of Poems, by Bessie Woodson Yancey. Washington, D. C., The Associated Publishers (c1939).
62 pages.
ABSpl   DHU   HE   NYPLS

YEISER, IDABELLE.

Moods, A Book of Verse, by Idabelle Yeiser, with pen sketches by Lindsey B. Murdah. Philadelphia, Pa., The Colony Press. 1937.
88 pages.
DHU

SELECTED REFERENCES ON THE HISTORY AND
CRITICISM OF NEGRO POETRY

BRAWLEY, BENJAMIN G.—Early Negro American Writers. Chapel Hill, The University of North Carolina Press, 1935. 305 pages.

BRAWLEY, BENJAMIN G.—The Negro Genius. New York, Dodd, Mead and Co., 1940. 366 pages.

BRAWLEY, BENJAMIN G.—Paul Laurence Dunbar, Poet of His People. Chapel Hill, The University of North Carolina Press, 1936. 159 pages.

BRAWLEY, BENJAMIN G.—Three Negro Poets: Horton, Mrs. Harper and Whitman. Journal of Negro History, 2: 384-92, O 1917.

BROWN, STERLING A.—The Blues as Folk Poetry. In Folk—Say, A Regional Miscellany, 1930, edited by B. A. Botkin. Norman, University of Oklahoma Press, 1930. p. 324-339.

BROWN, STERLING A(LLEN).—The Negro Caravan, Writings by American Negroes. Selected and edited by Sterling A. Brown, Arthur P. Davis and Ulysses Lee. New York, The Dryden Press, (c1941). 1082 pages.
ABSpl DHU DLC HPDpl NYPLS

BROWN, STERLING A.—Negro Poetry and Drama. Washington, D. C., The Associates in Negro Folk Education, 1937. 142 pages.

BROWN, STERLING A.—An Outline for the Study of The Poetry of American Negroes. New York, Harcourt, Brace & Co., 1931.

CALVERTON, V. F.—Anthology of American Negro Literature. New York, The Modern Library, 1929. 535 pages.

ELEAZER, ROBERT B., COMP.—Singers in the Dawn: A Brief Supplement to the Study of American Literature, compiled by Robert B. Eleazer. Atlanta, Ga., Published by Conference on Education and Race Relations, (1934). 23 pages.

ELY, EFFIE SMITH.—American Negro Poetry. Christian Century, 40: 366-7, Mr. 22, 1923.

GREEN, ELIZABETH LAY.—The Negro in Contemporary American Literature. Chapel Hill, The University of North Carolina Press, 1928. 94 pages.

HEARTMAN, CHARLES F.—Phillis Wheatley (Phillis Peters); a Critical Attempt and Bibliography of Her Writings. New York, printed for the Author, 1915.

HEARTMAN, CHARLES F.—Six Broadsides Relating to Phillis Wheatley. n.p. Privately printed, 1915.

HEATH, PHOEBE ANNIE.—Negro Poetry as an Historical Record. Vassar Journal of Undergraduate Studies, 3:34-52, My 1928.

KERLIN, ROBERT T.—Contemporary Poetry of the Negro. (Hampton, Va., Press of the Hampton Normal and Agricultural Institute, 1921). 23 pages.

KERLIN, ROBERT T.—Negro Poets and Their Poems. Washington, D. C., The Associated Publishers, 1923. 285 pages.

KERLIN, ROBERT T.
    Present Day Negro Poets. Southern Workman. 49:543, D 1920.

LAWSON, VICTOR.
    Dunbar Critically Examined. Washington, D. C., The Associated Publishers, c1941. 151 pages.

LOCKE, ALAIN L.
    Dry Fields and Green Pastures. Opportunity Journal of Negro Life, 28: 4-10, 28, Ja 1940.

LOGGINS, VERNON.
    The Negro Author: His Development in America. New York, Columbia University Press, 1931. 480 pages.

MORTON, LENA BEATRICE.
    Negro Poetry in America. Boston, Mass., The Stratford Co., 1925. 71 pages.

REDDING, J. SAUNDERS.
    To Make a Poet Black. Chapel Hill, The University of North Carolina Press, 1939. 142 pagess.

SCHOMBURG, ARTHUR A.
    A Bibliographical Checklist of American Negro Poetry. New York, Charles F. Heartman, 1916. 57 pages.

TAUSSIG, XHARLOTTE E.
    The New Negro as Revealed in His Poetry. Opportunity, Journal of Negro Life. 5: 108-111, April 1927.

TINKER, EDWARD LAROCQUE.
    Les Cenelles, Afro-French Poetry in Louisiana. New York, 1930. Reprinted from the Colophon, Pt. 3, Sept. 1913.

WEEKS, STEPHEN B.
    George Moses Horton; Slave Poet. Southern Workman, 43: 571, October 1914.

WEGELIN, OSCAR.
Jupiter Hammon, American Negro Poet. Selections from His Writings and a Bibliography, with five facsimiles. New York, Printed for C. F. Heartman, 1915.

WHITE, NEWMAN I.
American Negro Poetry. South Atlantic Quarterly 20: 304-22, O 1921.

WHITE, NEWMAN I. and JACKSON, WALTER C.—An Anthology of Verse by American Negroes, edited with a critical introduction, biographical sketches of the authors, and bibliographical notes by N. I. White. Durham, N. C., Trinity College Press, 1924. 250 pages.

WHITE, NEWMAN I.—Racial Feeling in Negro Poetry. South Atlantic Quarterly, 21: 14-29, Ja 1922.

WOOD, CLEMENT.—Negro Songs, An Anthology, Girard, Kansas, Haldeman Julius Co., 1924. 64 pages.